Why Do I Have to Think Like a **Man**?

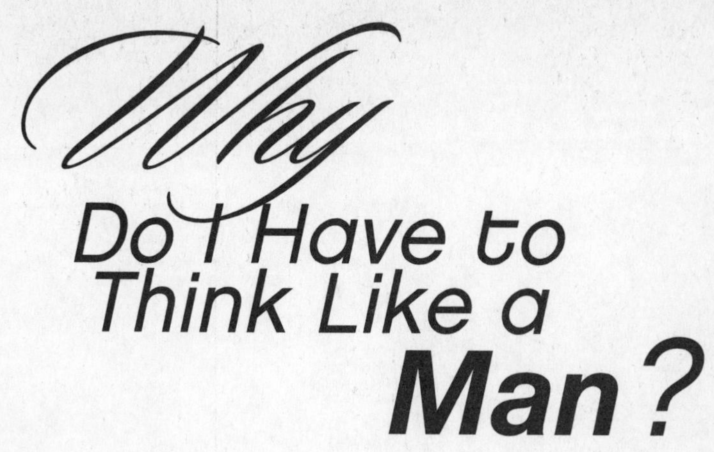

Why Do I Have to Think Like a Man?

How to Think Like a Lady and Still Get the Man

Shanae Hall and Rhonda Frost

Health Communications, Inc.
Deerfield Beach, Florida

www.hcibooks.com

Library of Congress Cataloging-in-Publication Data
is available through the Library of Congress.

ISBN-13: 978-0-7573-1792-7 (Paperback)
ISBN-10: 978-0-7573-1792-8 (Paperback)
ISBN-13: 978-0-7573-1793-4 (ePub)
ISBN-10: 978-0-7573-1793-6 (ePub)

Publisher: Health Communications, Inc.
3201 S.W. 15th Street
Deerfield Beach, FL 33442-8190

Dedication

This book is dedicated to all women who are ready to ask themselves, "What could I have done differently to get what I wanted out of the relationship?" or "How do I heal now that I'm out of it?"

To my three loving kids, Nya, Iliah, and my handsome son, Cory Jr. Thank you for being my motivation to continue to live life to the fullest.
—Shanae Hall

To my children—Shanae, Janelle, Moriah, and Gibraun—and to my mom Bonnie who taught me in many ways, unbeknownst to her, how to strive for better.
—Rhonda Frost

Contents

Preface

Ladies, when you were born, God gave you a mind to think with and a heart to feel with. He gave you intuition to use as your personal crystal ball to see through truth and lies, as well as the good and bad in people. As you grew up, your mind and your intuition were either nurtured or stifled by events and people. If they were nurtured, they became more keen and aware. If they were stifled, they became dull and you tended not to trust them anymore. Our hearts were either well cared for and uplifted through loving connections and respect or broken by those who would look to decieve and hurt us. Too many broken hearts from lies and pain lead to a lack of trust in self and others. This renders your natural instincts helpless and places you in danger. This breakdown leads to poor choices in men and relationships and lowers self-esteem.

For too many of us, this is our truth. We have given up our power and are lost. We no longer trust our God-given instincts or intuition to provide guidance. We have forgotten who we were created to be and what our purpose is.

We wrote this book to remind you of who you are and to get you to see your greatness again.

Each of us has experienced relationship love, happiness, and pain. Some of us know what it is like to try to hold on to people who we loved who didn't love us back. Many of us can relate to making the decision to let go of relationships and dating habits that no longer serve our greater purpose. Here you will see some of those stories.

If you are a reader of self-help or relationship books, you have undoubtedly heard of Dr. John Gray, the author of seventeen relationship books, that have sold 50 million books worldwide, including *Men Are from Mars, Women Are from Venus* (New York: HarperCollins, 1992), the book that told us that men and women think differently. Perhaps you have heard of George Gilder, who authored *Men and Marriage* (Gretna: Pelican, 1986), the man who stated in no uncertain terms, "In virtually every known society, sex is regarded either as a grant by the woman to the man or as an object of male seizure. In most societies, the man has to pay for it with gifts or service." His book goes on to say, "The male role in marriage . . . in every known human society, is to provide for women and children. In order to marry, in fact, . . . almost every human society first requires the man to prove his capacity to maintain the woman." Or how about Hill Harper, the Harvard-educated actor turned author who wrote the popular dating book *The Conversation* (Penguin, 2009), who gave us a peek into dialogue about many subjects from black men dating white women to sistas and their attitudes. Each of these men boldly offers a peek into a male perspective on relationships. Then we have Steve Harvey who gave us *Act Like a Lady, Think Like a Man* (New York: HarperCollins, 2009) who told us many of the same things found in the earlier books, as well as how to think and how many days to wait before sex. He has promised us that if we play our cards right, we can learn how to find a man, get a man, and keep a man by following just a few crucial steps, straight from the handbook of the original player himself. His book got many of us talking and thinking a whole lot about these ideas, relationships, and dating. We'll talk more about this book later.

Ladies, to keep it all the way real, no one book has all the answers. If it did, there wouldn't be a need for a new book, and there wouldn't be news specials or forums on why women can't find a husband or keep a man, even with all the knowledge and great advice that is out there. So why us, why now? Because it is time—it is time for some real girlfriend talk about the BS and about the state of our situation.

This book is not written by a guru or self-proclaimed expert. The reason this book is relevant is because it is "straight talk, no chaser" (as Gena Pitts named it while discussing our book in *Pro-Sports Wives Magazine,* December 2009) complete with dating revelations from women who look, think, and act like you; who have been through what you have been through and have decided enough is enough and that we can do better. No, we are not a man, so we don't think like one, nor will we ever. We are emotional, strong, loving creators of this earth. Without whom nothing comes to life.

This book of personal stories, interviews, quotes, and revelations will reinforce for you that our views resemble yours. Our walk, hurt, and pain will look and feel exactly like what you have been through. Our recovery and change is something palpable. Something you can feel, believe, and perhaps have experienced.

If what you are currently doing, reading, and saying is working for you, great! Keep doing it. If not, and you want to see a moving picture of relationship lessons from women as well as hear men's comments and witness revolutionary advice that will work if you use it, then turn the page and let's get this change started. As Brahma the king of the gods so eloquently stated to Siddhartha the enlightened one, *"some of us perhaps have only a little dirt in our eyes and could awaken if we only heard 'This' story."* Let's awaken together.

Remember, information and advice should be consumed like you eat fish: eat the meat and take out the bones (my sister Carolyn gave me that one). Keep and use what works for you from all sources, spit out the rest and move on to the next source. Know that all the knowledge in the world only helps if you apply it to your situation, otherwise its just information. So open the door to *Why Do I Have to Think Like a Man? How to Think Like a Lady and Still Get the Man* and let's get this party "with a purpose" started.

Acknowledgments

I want to send a special thank you to all the men who took time out of their day to be interviewed (more aptly, *grilled*) by us. I must give a huge thank you to Cedric The Entertainer for being one of the most honest men that I know, and for the wonderful endorsement. Today, I am a better and wiser person because of the men that God has put in my life.
—Shanae Hall

A heartfelt thank you goes out to all the men in my life who opened my eyes to the truth about how men really think. I want to thank my daughter Shanae for her strength, courage, wisdom, humor, and blunt talks about dating standards, even when it was uncomfortable. It is because of her, in part, that I changed how I dated, raised the bar, and reaffirmed my self-worth. I want to thank "Speedy" for taking the time to sit down and talk to us, for his honesty in sharing the raw, uncut version of relationships between men and women and how most men think. I want to thank my daughter Janelle for asking the questions. I also want to thank Roderick for his impact on my life and his support of this project.
—Rhonda Frost

Introduction

Shanae

When I was thirteen, my mom received a job promotion that required our family to move from El Centro to Bakersfield, California. I was entering high school in a new city, but I must admit, Bakersfield was a step up from El Centro. At Stockdale High, located in a dusty town in the middle of California where only a handful of black people lived, I met the man who would help mold my current vision of what a man should and should not be. If I believed in love at first sight then, I would tell you that is what I felt when I met Cory Hall.

I clearly recall standing in the hallway my freshman year, socializing with some of my classmates, when this guy walked up on the right side of me. He was so handsome. I had never seen a man who made me stop and stare before, but this guy did. I asked around to find out who he was and if he had a girlfriend. I was told that his name was Cory, he played football, and that he was either very shy or gay because he didn't socialize with females much. I later found out he wasn't gay and he was asking about me, too. He was too shy to ask me for my number, so he gave his to my friend who gave it to me. We began talking on the phone a lot and spending small amounts of time together outside of class. I told my mom and everyone I knew that I was going to marry him! I didn't know when, I just knew he would be the "one" at some point in my life.

Cory and I went on our first date when I was fifteen, and I quickly learned that boys will only become men if you force them to. Assuming I was like the other girls he had gone out with before, Cory thought he could take me on a date without any money—basically on a free date. Since I knew, even as a young girl, *never* to go on a date without any cash, I usually kept fifty dollars in my purse. I also knew that if a guy wanted to date me, he had better come correct.

When Cory and I pulled up to the window at the drive-in movie theater, the attendant said, "Seven dollars, please." Cory looked at me, and I looked back at him. Without even thinking of reaching into my purse to pull out my money, I told him to take me home and said, "Don't ever go out with me with the expectation that I will pay!"

Instead of taking me home, Cory drove us to his house to get a small check his dad had sent him. He then drove to Liquor King (a liquor store in the neighborhood that would cash checks) got his money, and drove us back to the drive-in. Once we were settled in, I showed Cory that I had money, and reiterated to him that I was not that kind of girl. “You can be a star athlete and one of the most beautiful men that I have ever seen, but you have to understand that it still costs to date me.” That moment was a building block in the foundation of our relationship. Cory now understood that if he wanted me to be his girl, he had to be a man when he was with me. We never had that discussion again.

After high school, we moved in together and shared most of the bills. Because I worked at a bank and made more than his $526 football scholarship check, I bought most of the groceries and took care of the miscellaneous things that we needed. Cory always said, “When I make it to the NFL your only job will be the house, our kids, and being my wife,” and he kept his word. In 1999, Cory was the second pick of the third round in the NFL draft. A few weeks after the draft, he sent me a couple dozen roses with a note that said, “Yes, I will marry you!” I called and said, “Where is the ring?” He said, “I haven’t got my signing bonus yet, but as soon as it comes, I got you.” This is how my life began as an NFL wife.

Rhonda

I have spent half of my life either married or seeking a committed relationship. Some of the men I dated were decent, and some were just downright awful. I have stuck with guys who were broke and broken in spirit. I’ve been with the guy who needed a loan to help pay his bills, the guy who needed help getting a cell phone because his credit was bad, and the one who was always overdrawn on his account. Guess what? I loaned them money and paid some of their bills. Why? Because I could and wanted to show my "independence." I have had the liar, the cheater, and some who were a combination of both. Back then it didn't matter. I was just happy to have a man. I never thought about standards. Without an example of a "good man," I simply followed my heart and became attached to what I thought was love, in the name of love. The end result was lose-lose all the way around.

I had two children by the time I was seventeen years old. As a young, African American teenage mom from a broken home, the odds were stacked against me. Pushing through the odds, I obtained a job in Corporate America and worked diligently. And the hard work paid off. I was promoted every two to three years and proved to myself that I was in charge of my life. I controlled my own destiny. By the time I was thirty-two years old, I was the epitome of *Ms. Independent*. I had the new house, the new Rover, the designer shoes and clothes, and the well-dressed children. My relationships, however, were in complete turmoil. I still had a long way to go before I would figure it all out.

Shanae and I hope that as you read this book, you will see the message behind the stories, laugh at the obvious, and be relieved to know that you are not the only one experiencing certain situations in your relationships. We also hope our stories will inspire and encourage you to take better care of yourself. Our ultimate goal is to help you build yourself up, to help eliminate unnecessary dating drama in your life, and encourage you to establish healthier relationships overall.

Shanae

What do men really want? That's the billion-dollar question. It's probably safe to assume that if anyone knew, Bill Clinton wouldn't have risked impeachment; John Wayne Bobbitt would still have an intact penis; Steve McNair would be headed to the Pro Bowl; David Carradine would be working on his next film; and Neil Diamond, Michael Jordan, Mel Gibson, Steven Spielberg, and countless other men would be hundreds of millions of dollars richer. So, we won't even attempt to answer that question.

What we hope you will learn from this book is how to get the most out of your relationships and to explore what you need to work on within yourself to achieve this goal. Truly, you are the only one who can change yourself and therefore your circumstances.

Let's get started.

Dating Game 101

Have you ever had a relationship that fell apart for no obvious reason? Ever found out that the man you had fallen in love with or liked a whole lot was not the guy you thought he was? Ever been lied to, cheated on, or misled by a man? Have you ever gone through any of these scenarios and quite simply couldn't think of anything else to say but, "What the hell just happened?" If you answered "yes" to any of these questions, we can relate because so have we! Many times we have asked, what the hell is going on in relationships today? Why should we have to *"think like a man"* when dating? Is that the only way to find relationship bliss? What do men want and what does it take to find love, commitment, and honesty in a relationship? Does it even exist? We found that in many of our dating experiences, the stories were the same. Whether the guys were rich or middle class, young or old, well educated or not, the bottom line was all men wanted something from us but many didn't want to give anything in return. Men wanted our goodies and our time for free.

So what do we do? How do we set our standards so that we experience a win-win situation every time? How do we ensure that no matter how it turns out, we can walk away feeling like we spent our time well and benefited from the dating experience?

First, you have to know your value as a woman. That means feeling comfortable expecting a particular level of treatment from anyone you encounter. God created us in His image, which is greatness, and we have to expect that same level of greatness from anyone we allow in our lives. Sadly, we can't tell you how many conversations we've had with men and women who have equated having these expectations with some form of prostitution. Our question is: *"So what is it called when we just lie down, expect nothing, and get nothing? What's the label for that?"* In our opinion, that example is just a fraction of the brainwashing that men have been able to get away with for decades. The sad part is that many of us have bought into it. Men today would like us to believe that we want too much if we ask for anything other than sex.

Second, don't let your independence get in the way of letting a man be a man. There are women who are proud to say, "I don't want anything from a man!" These women relate well to the lyrics of Ne-Yo's 2008 song, "Miss Independent," or Jamie Foxx's lyrics to "She Got Her Own" (the remix).

Ladies, please! As independent women ourselves, this is bullshit. We could sell ten million copies of this book and our position would still be the same. If you're sleeping in it, "you" bought it; if you're driving in it, "you" bought it; and if you're eating it, best believe you bought it. Men have women thinking this *mess* is fly. We fully embrace and support independent women who have their own money and are able to do nice things for their men, but we are also strong advocates of allowing men the opportunity to demonstrate their manhood by serving as a provider. We invite you to explore this in more detail with us in later chapters.

THE WORLD ACCORDING TO STEVE

We would be remiss if we didn't again mention Steve Harvey's book, *Act Like a Lady, Think Like a Man*. We certainly read the book and are sure many of you did, too. We want to take time to thank Mr. Harvey for the book that got us all talking about relationships. He raised some interesting topics and gave some useful advice. But there was some advice that was suspect and made us wonder *WTF*? (Throughout this book,we use the acronym WTF which means "What the fu*k?" Sometimes this is the only comment to best describe the situation!). To be clear, we are not Steve Harvey haters, we respect his hustle and his accomplishments. We simply beg to differ with some of the advice in his book, and since we live in America where women can actually disagree with men and still live, we thought we would voice our concerns, compare our real life experieces, and talk about it a little.

In this book, we are going to show you by example why the time is right for change. This book is going to debunk some of the myths you have heard and give you what

Steve (and no other man for that matter) could not—an uncensored, woman's view on dating. In just a few short pages you will find real stories and reasons why you must reclaim your power. These will be raw and uncut depictions of married and single women committing mistakes, selling themselves short, hearing but not listening to the men they date and not heeding the obvious warnings.

No *man* can ever tell you what it's like to date a man, trust his words, invest your time, invest your emotions, then sleep with him, only to be left hanging—or find that he doesn't feel the same about you anymore or that he suddenly needs "time to think things through" as he vanishes out of your life and into the next woman's bed. No *man* can ever tell you how it feels to meet a guy who says to you, "I am single looking for my queen" only to discover after dating for several months, he is actually married.

This book will be like watching a powerful, drama-filled, action-packed movie. While reading it, you just might see yourself or someone you know in the starring role making the same mistakes over and over again, being victimized until one day they wake up, look in the mirror, and realize they have the kryptonite—the power to turn it all around.

About men and their double standards . . . Recently, my girlfriend experienced a situation that reminded her how guys are very confident about stating their standards and could care less how it makes women feel. I was in Las Vegas for the Mayweather fight. I brought a girlfriend with me and met up with one of my boyfriend's friends. My friend is a very pretty girl with beautiful long black hair (it's real), straight teeth, and great skin—just a cute girl. When I introduced them, she noticed that the guy didn't really even look at her; she was left wondering WTH? A few days later, when I saw him, I asked why he had acted like that. He said, "Because she didn't have hips or a butt." Huh? Wow! Now, if we were to say, "Naw, I can't talk to that guy because I heard his penis is the size of my thumb," or "His bank account balance looks like a bad credit score," then we'd be called all kinds of bad names. These are the kind of double-standards we are talking about. Men have no problem with their very clear and oftentimes superficial standards for women, but if we let them know what we want straight up (like asking them to take us shopping, help us with a car repair, be a provider, etc.) then we're "doing too much" or being "too demanding." Obviously this game needs changing!

Quite honestly, after you read some of these true events, you'll see that there are no better words to express the emotion than WTF. Some of the names have been changed to protect the guilty and the innocent, who are our friends and family. Sit back, relax, and enjoy.

Part One

What Do Men Really Want?

Chapter 1:

You Can’t Change Him

Don't hate the player; hate the game. It's not the man that makes the difference, it's how you deal with the man that makes the difference between heartbreak and a mutually beneficial situation. First off, women need to stop walking around with blinders on. If you see that the man of your dreams is promiscuous, a flirt, a liar, or selfish, he isn't going to change because you gave him some (that is, had sex with him) or because you gave birth to his child. Let's be realistic. If he is trifling, that is his character, *period*. Now, most men do grow up at some point, and the things they desire from their women can change. But for the most part, barring divine intervention, a strong desire to change, or intensive therapy, a man's character is consistent throughout his life.

Shanae

October 2006, my birthday weekend, my mom bought us tickets to see the Laffapalooza comedy show held in Atlanta every year. The plan was dinner, the concert, and (hopefully) the after party. So, after the show, I went up to the emcee of the show and asked if I could get tickets to the after party. He asked who I was there with, I pointed to my mom, he smiled, then promptly led us backstage.

While backstage I met a man, who I will call "Mark." He was funny, friendly, and seemed very sweet.

Mark and I exchanged numbers and stayed in contact. We talked on the phone, text messaged each other, i-chatted, e-mailed, and saw each other in different cities as mere friends. There were several nights we stayed together and slept in the same bed without having sex.

One night, I visited Mark at his home in Los Angeles. It was a beautiful mansion on the hill. He had just moved into the house so there wasn't much furniture, except for a few beds and a flat-screen TV. We talked about his plans to decorate and how happy he was to have found that place. We stayed up all night laughing and talking. Around 5:30 in the morning, we took his Hummer to the top of the hill and watched the sunrise. It was so romantic. Afterward, we returned to Mark's house and slept. We literally just went to sleep—no kissing, no making out.

Mark and I established a really nice friendship in a short amount of time. I have to admit, over the course of our friendship, I saw Mark with many different women. I don't think that I ever saw him with the same girl twice. Yet, it never bothered me because we were just friends, and all I thought about were his great qualities, and how humorous, nurturing, smart, and talented he was. Then one day the dynamics of our relationship changed, and I knew Mark could "get it." He was celebrating his birthday in Miami, and I decided to join him at the party along with a host of other guests. All of Mark's family came together to celebrate his birthday and, for some reason, it made him very emotional. He was crying while holding his mom's hand and then I started crying. It was a very moving moment. We embraced for a moment and wiped the tears away and the party commenced. We danced, drank, and had an incredible time. As the night began to wind down, we shared our first real kiss, and other passionate events (can't kiss and tell). When the night was over, we were too intoxicated to escalate our intimacy to the next level. I gave him a soft kiss on the lips, went to my room alone, and fell asleep.

We still saw each other regularly, but our next one-on-one time didn't take place until the following year. Shortly after I had moved to Los Angeles, I showed up unannounced at his office, as I had sometimes done in the past. On this particular day, he had to leave early and head to the studio to finish up some work. He asked me if I wanted to accompany him. "Sure," I answered. We were at the studio for about three hours when he told me he had to go to a meeting. He invited me to dinner at a restaurant in Santa Monica, where he was supposed to have his meeting. The dinner was great; he was wonderful company and we had a really nice time. I felt good about meeting his acquaintances. Things felt right. At the end of our great evening, we returned to the studio to finish listening to his upcoming CD. Suddenly, he walked over to a keyboard and began playing and singing a song he had written. It was so beautiful. I thought I had died and gone to heaven. I was completely caught up in the moment.

When the date was over, Mark gave me a kiss on my lips and on both butt cheeks. That was it. The date was over. And I left with a feeling of euphoria. I was in love, or at least "in strong like." Several months elapsed before the opportunity for romance arose again. This time it was far less romantic and far more natural and spontaneous. Okay, I will stop playing and get to the good stuff. One night in Mark's office, he and I were talking about the *American Idol* show that had just aired. It was late and I had just begun to get my things together to leave. I walked over to Mark and gave him a hug and a kiss on the cheek as I always did. But this time it was different. We made eye contact with one another and began kissing passionately. His hand slowly moved up my back as we made our way to the sofa. . . . at least that is how it went in my mind. In real life, next thing I knew we were butt naked on the desk, and I was wondering why he still had on his mid-calf socks. (smile)

After knowing each other almost three years, we finally made love. There is something really provocative about having sex in an office. To this day, I can't walk past Mark's office without thinking about all the positions we were able to find in such a small area.

On my way home, I was all smiles. It was sensual and impulsive. I had no regrets. After this, I just knew we would start spending more time together and talking on the phone more. That is not what happened. Four days after our erotic sex, he sent me a text message that read "good night" signed with a smiley face. Not a call, to ask if I was okay. A text message! And four days later! Ain't that about a bitch?! Now keep in mind, I held out for three years! So much for "Ninety-Day Rule!" It's comical now but back then, I was kinda hurt. The moral of this story is that you need to see the man and situation for what they are—call a spade a spade. I knew early on that Mark saw different women, but for some reason I thought after three years, our relationship would be different. If a man changes into a diamond (aka a keeper), it won't be because of what you did or didn't do. It will be because it was just that time in his life to change his ways or settle down. It will have little to do with you personally, except that you arrived at the right time and place in his life.

Now let's talk about the part women play in men becoming "players." My story shows how, in certain situations, women contribute to this whole phenomenon. All too often, we opt to look past the warning signs that are directly in front of our faces. Instead, we see only what we want to see. As women, we see in men whatever we are missing or desire the most, even if it's not really there. In this scenario with Mark, he was nurturing, kind, humble, and different from what I was used to seeing in a man who had "made it." After being married to someone who had "made it" in the NFL but who acted the opposite of Mark, it was not only refreshing, it was captivating. Mark showed me what I wanted to see. You can "have it all" and still show kindness, respect, and love to those around you. I was smitten by this realization.

Women often look for a man who possesses what they lacked in the previous relationship; whether it's money, a good sex partner, or encouragement. We seek what we're personally missing from the men we date. Unfortunately, we women tend to confuse sex with love. They are not the same thing. If done right, sex makes your whole body tingle from head to toe while love lifts your confidence and self-esteem, making you feel safe and warm. We have to get clear about this.

It's our turn to take better control of the situations we are in and stop blaming the men we choose to deal with. It's time to take credit for our "good picks" and responsibility for the "bad ones." Some women want to blame everyone around them for the type of relationships they are in. Stop it. We are going to stop squinting our eyes, looking the other way, and also stop calling spades, diamonds. There is a difference and you are about to learn it.

Clearly, it is our responsibility to set goals and establish standards. To drive the point home, how about the following example? A male friend of mine who I'll call

Curtis always says, “If I don’t hit it after the first three dates, I’m done.” What if women started saying, “If I don’t get a rent check within the first three dates, I’m done?” Very few people would be having sex, that’s for sure! Sex would be limited to the rich and those willing to concede to this new rule. What I’m telling you is that men should have to work harder than three dates to get some of the goodies. If an overweight forty-seven-year-old man with eight kids, very little savings, and a 1992 BMW can have these kinds of standards, what does that say about women today? The crazy thing is he gets women all too often! What do our standards look like? Oh, my God! Just think about it. If we see a man that is even close to being “in shape” with a few pesos on him, we treat him like Jesus on Resurrection Day (there is only one). We give him all the breaks, all the credit, and we hang in there like there’s no tomorrow, no matter how he makes us feel. Is that his fault?

There are over 315 million people in the United States and some of these people are single men. You don’t have to settle ladies. If we are dense enough to believe we have to fight, settle, and compromise our wants and needs for one man, shame on us. Of the other 314,999,999 people left, surely we can find one that will treat us right, call us after we have sex with him, make sure we are okay, take us on dates, or bother to ask about our families, our children, our lives, and all that other good stuff that we like. I can’t blame the recipient, I blame the giver. We have men believing that *they* are God's gift to this earth and that we will fight for them no matter how they treat us. It's time to reconstruct the game and raise our self-esteem.

One conversation that I had, hammered this message home for me. I confided in a mature female friend about something Mark had done, but before I could begin my story, she asked, "Does he make sure you eat, put a roof over your head, and put money in your pocket?" I said, "No." She asked,"Does he claim you as his girl?" I had to answer honestly. I said, "No." She said, "Then I don't want to hear it! If it's not all about you, then he's not for you, so let it go." That was real talk. Honesty and self-reflection are the most difficult things to face, but they result in the greatest growth.

So now I say the same thing to you. If you are looking for more than sex and it's not all about you, then keep it moving. We have given too much control to men who don't deserve it. We fail to realize that what's between our legs makes us extra powerful and we have given it away all too easily for far too long. Today is the day that we raise the bar, ladies.

Since the main goal of 99 percent of the men on planet earth is to have sex with someone, it's our turn to figure out what we want and need from men as well. What is our main goal? There used to be a time when women just wanted to be loved, protected, nurtured, and provided for.

Many of us still maintain such a dream. However, because of the changes in our society and the ruthlessness of some men, we too have to change and adjust to the new rules that men are playing by.

My ex-husband says, "I trick a little so they can trick a lot," and that really didn't make sense to me until one day when a woman I know named Beverly told me about a recent relationship tragedy she had. She said, "Shanae, I met this great guy. He is tall, has beautiful chocolate skin, makes me laugh, treats my daughter like a princess, gives her an allowance, takes us out, and treats me like a queen. He rubs my feet and the sex is amazing." I said, "For real? How long have you been dating him?" She said, "Almost three weeks." I said, "Call me in three months, and then tell me how great he is." After a month, Beverly called and said they were moving in together. Now Beverly had been living in the house that her recently deceased grandfather left her. It was paid in full—no notes, no liens, nothing. But her new boyfriend convinced her they needed to upgrade to this beautiful, new rental for twenty-five hundred dollars a month. Trustingly, Beverly said, "Okay." (I'm sure she was thinking her man was going to take care of her, no big deal.) Beverly's new boyfriend also asked her to put the new house in her name because his credit was "messed up." This is a red flag that even Ray Charles could see, but she went along with it. A week later, Beverly called me and said they were engaged.

I knew something wasn't right, but I told her *congratulations* and asked about the bachelorette party and wedding. A week later, Beverly called and told me she had bought a Mercedes-Benz in her name and put his name on the title. A few weeks after that, she called to tell me her man and the Benz were missing. Weeks go by no call, e-mail, or text message. Beverly was losing her mind. He finally called from a blocked number and explained to her that he had driven to Atlanta to visit his kids. After all the dust settled, Beverly learned that he was staying with his baby's mama in Atlanta. I said, "Girl, you better sell that ring."

Oh, I forgot to mention that he presented her with a ring at her job. He had red roses, got down on one knee in the presence of her coworkers and proposed. Oh, the ring was in her name, too! WTF?

What should you learn from this example? Open your eyes and pay attention to all of the red flags that people show you. Listen to a man's words, observe his actions, and see if they match. If a man is doing too much, asking for too much, and puttin' it on thick early, watch out! People can say anything! Remember that a man who cheats, lies, and has multiple women is disconnected on so many levels that he lacks the ability to become emotionally attached. Be on the lookout for this type of guy. Honestly, I was mad as hell at the jerk who hurt Beverly, but I was more disappointed for her, because I wanted her to be happy and he let her down.

I think it is safe to say that many of us have had our own *"wow"* stories that we would like to forget, most of us have been there. Ladies, we tend to be needy at times, or maybe some of us have always been needy. Look around you, or just look in the mirror. How many women do you know who always have a story about being played, cheated on, mistreated, or abused in some manner? How many? Did it ever cross your mind that maybe it isn't the man's fault for being an asshole, but our fault for allowing him to treat us in a way that doesn't make us feel good?

Of course they are going to be great for the first three dates. They have a goal in mind. We have allowed ourselves to become the prey. I can't count how many times I have read or heard that "men are hunters by nature." It is their natural instinct to look for prey. Too often, we put our head in the sand and behave like we don't know why these people continue to come into our lives and cause us pain, disrespect us, and leave us with unmet needs. Well, let me help you out. It's because you (and I) let them! That's that. I don't have an in-depth answer or the desire to give you some long psychological explaination. Ultimately, it's because we let them.

Now it is our job to figure out *why* we let them. Is it because we are needy? Do we have low self-esteem and don't know it? Are we trying to replace a male figure in our life that we never had? Do we not feel worthy or powerful? Do we not feel beautiful or healthy? Whatever it is, you and I need to look inside ourselves and find it, admit it, then fix it, so we can decrease our chances of accepting the same crap again.

My mom always tells me that I am too hard on guys. My younger sister, Moriah, always laughs and says, "I feel sorry for any guy that likes you, Nae." The truth of the matter is, she doesn't have to feel sorry for them. They won't be around me long enough to get hurt or develop any kind of emotional attachment because if something doesn't sound or look right to me, they're gone. These days, I call it like it is, and often people don't like what I have to say. But the truth of the matter is that the people in my life now are of far more character, and I am being treated better than ever.

I have been around professional athletes and entertainers for the past decade. I have seen the best and the worst that the male species has to offer. What I know for sure is that men are only going to treat you as good as you demand! Call it being a gold digger, high-maintenance, streetwalker, or whatever other creative words that men can think of, it really doesn't matter; you need to establish what you want and need from the relationship from the beginning.

When you meet a man you like and he is interested in you, do yourself a favor, don't look at him like he's the "one." Look at him like he's a man with an agenda and possible potential. Give him ample time to show himself to you. If he turns out to be the one, great!

Okay, here we go.

Dating 201

You should place every guy you meet into one of the following four categories:

Category 1: Lose my number
Category 2: Friends
Category 3: Friends with mutual benefits
Category 4: My man

If you are anything like me, you have an idea of what category a man will fall into between the first hello and the second conversation, assuming he doesn't do anything to mess it up when he opens his mouth.

Category 1 Lose My Number

If you go out on a date and the person you are with says something that rubs you the wrong way, or does something that comes across as a red flag, evaluate it, ask questions to clarify it, and if he can't clear up the misunderstanding, put him in the "lose my number" category immediately following the date. You don't necessarily have to tell him while you are on the date, just make a mental note.

Here are a few examples of a "lose my number" guy:

• He asks you to pay the bill or to leave the tip (this is a big "oh hell no" on the first date).
• He tells you he's on probation for beating up his ex-girlfriend.
• He talks about his ex-girlfriend the entire night.
• He continues to talk about sex when you are obviously not interested.

I'm sure you get the point. You can't change him, so if you know in your heart and mind this ain't gonna work, keep it moving.

Category 2 Friends

This is the guy whose company you love, but you just know he's not your type. He may be too short, too corny, has too many chicks, or too many teeth missing. Whatever it is you didn't like at the first introduction will come back to haunt you if you try to force a relationship. Keep him as your platonic buddy and keep looking.

Category 3 Friends with Benefits

This can be tricky. You have to be mentally prepared to enter into this category. This type of relationship means you both are getting what you need out of the situation but you understand you have no commitment. Most of the time this is a person you want to have a real relationship with and are likely already sleeping with, but there is something or someone standing in the way. Most men in this category are married, have a live-in girlfriend or baby mama, are not ready to settle down, or some combination thereof. If you're not careful, you can easily end up with a broken heart. Keep dating other people. Don't settle down with a man who is only partially yours. That is a no-no. Keep dating other men! If you don't have a ring or a clear indication that you both have agreed to be monogamous, keep looking for the man that is right for you.

Time is the only thing that you can't replace or get back. If you are with a man for five years and you still have to ask him when he's going to give you a ring or when you're going to move in together, this is a clue that it will never be what you want it to be. You have to keep your options open. One day you will open your eyes and be past your prime, asking yourself why you settled for so many years with nothing to show for it. I know several women who are faithful to married men or stopped dating because their boyfriend of a month asked them to stop seeing other people. You should be thinking like Beyoncé, when she so boldly proclaimed, *"If you like it, then you shoulda put a ring on it!"* Until then, you need to look at his ass the same way he is looking at you. What can he do for you and how soon can you get it? Trust me, in his mind he is definitely thinking, *"Can I hit it from the back?"* I wonder if her "head" game is right. *"Does her body look good naked?"*—if he doesn't already know. This is how it works. Also, never ask or expect anything up front from the man you are dating, let him ask first (and trust me, he will). No naked pictures without a date first. Most of you know what I am talking about. Everyone wants a picture sent to their phone or e-mail these days. No sex unless he has jumped through the ring of fire to convince you that he is worth entering into your temple. That means he should have impressed you with his character, flown you somewhere, taken you on some great trip of your choice, taken you on several dates, spent quality time with you, or otherwise done something of real quality or value other than told you how "fine" you are. The "Friends with Benefits" guy is not your man so don't delude yourself into thinking he is.

Category 4 My Man

What the hell is that? you may ask. Listen. If you have a ring, if he comes home to you, if he is faithful to you, if he makes sure that there is food on the table and clothes on your back (even if you can do it yourself), if he lifts your spirit up and respects you for the woman that you are, then he's your man. If not, well then, he's your man only when he's with you.

According to poet Carl Sandburg, "Time is the coin of your life. It is the only coin you have, but only you can determine how it will be spent; be careful lest you let other people spend it for you." Make sure everyone who gets a piece of your *coin* is worth it. Every person who you allow to come into your life should enhance it in some way. They should uplift you, make you smile, laugh, and feel good. And you should do the same for them. It really is a mutual thing.

Chapter 2
The Married Man

Statistically speaking, there is a 65 percent chance that the love of your life is having an affair. Be very suspicious.
Scott Dikkers

Shanae

Having been with my high school sweetheart my entire adult life and having been married for seven and a half of those years, I understand the energy that goes into keeping a family together. Marriage can be extremely hard without any external factors coming into play. But let's be real. Married men cheat like women change underwear, every day. I'm sure that most women are aware of that, and the ones who are still sitting at home with blinders on saying, "not my man," good for you. It may be better for you, not to know. For all the realists in the world, let's move on.

Why do married men cheat? Steve Harvey says the primary reason married men cheat is because "there are so many women willing to give themselves to a man who doesn't belong to them . . ." he goes on to say, "these are the women who have no standards and requirements and who suffer from serious self-esteem issues . . ." Incredulously, he then says, "if women took themselves out of the cheaters circle, the incidence of cheating would be cut seriously down?" (p. 106) Really? Wow! To keep it all the way real, we have to give him partial credit on that statement, there is some truth to that but let us get this right. Did he really convey that a married man who cheats is doing it because of the plethora of single low self-esteem women willing to give themselves to a married man? Let's examine this further, shall we? May I ask what moral obligation the married man has to his wife and family, to his God? Can we discuss the possibility that he is weak and may in fact suffer from *serious* low self-esteem issues himself? Or what if the mistress actually has high self-esteem and is smart enought to see this situation for what it is and is getting all her needs met through the relationship (e.g., bills paid, great sex, companionship . . .)? Or maybe, just maybe, we can look at the man just being greedy or him lacking respect for his wife or perhaps his ability to just say "no"? Is it really fair to place the entire burden of an affair with a married man, solely on the other woman? GTHOH (text messaging for "get the hell outta here" with that)!

While you are mulling that over, let's look at some analogies. So Steve says it's the women of the world's fault that guys cheat (primarily speaking of course). If they weren't there, men couldn't cheat. So let's apply this to thieves. A bank robber goes into the bank. Using the analogy we were given, if the bank didn't have money, the robber couldn't rob, right? Should banks find other places to store money so as to not tempt the thief? Sounds reasonable to me. What about the fat person who can't resist cake but wants to lose weight? Do we as a society need to stop baking cakes so the fat person can resist cakes or does the fat person need to have some discipline and desire to do right, eat right, and exercise? I am just sayin' this is the bullshit we are talking about!

Back to the question at hand, why do married men cheat? Is it lack of appreciation or affirmation? Not enough sex? Boredom? I don't know, and I don't care to dig into the male psyche to find out what they are missing or missed as a child that makes them believe it's okay to deceive the person they supposedly love. What bothers me is that women are always the angriest with the other woman. That is crazy to me. Married women, take time to remind your men that they have to respect you, and stop blaming other people for what is happening in your relationship.

I've heard married women say, "How could a woman date a married man?" My response is always, "How could a woman stay married to a man that she knows cheats on her?" I will never understand why a married woman would pick up the phone and call her husband's girlfriend (aka mistress) to "go off" on her! If you are married and calling your husband's mistress for any reason other than to confirm the truth or to get information to use in the divorce, you're delusional. The man married *you* and made his vows to *you*. He promised to "love, honor, and respect you til death do *you* part." I am saying this as a woman who was married and as a single woman; the "other woman" wasn't there that day.

Of the many excuses married men give as reasons to cheat, one is that their spouse will not have sex with them. Even though I am not an expert, I think it's safe to assume, this would be one of several valid issues likely to lead to an affair. I am going to biblical with you on this one, to drive home an important point as it relates to this . . . The Bible tells us it is not good that man should be alone: *"Let each man have his own wife and let each woman have her own husband. Let the husband render to his wife the affection due her, and likewise also the wife to her husband. The wife does not have authority over her own body, but the husband does . . . Do not deprive one another except with consent for a time that you may give yourselves to fasting and prayer; come together again so that Satan does not tempt you because of your lack of self-control* (I Corinthians 7:2-5; KJV)."

Wow! I have so many male friends who talk about their wives not having sex with them, or if they do have sex with them, they say it's like ringing a dinner bell—*ding, ding,* come and get it and hurry up, the clock is ticking. The feeling of someone having sex with you because they have to is completely different from making love. Whether you believe in God and the Bible or not, believe this ladies; if you don't have sex with your husband over time, someone else will! They won't care if he doesn't fold clothes or help with the kids. Not having sex with your man is the fastest way to run him into the arms of another woman. I have several married, male friends who talk to me about their problems. I listen, but, trust me, my comments to them aren't, "Oh, poor you!" I talk to them just like many of you have heard me talk on the radio or in real life, straight, raw, and uncut. And I will tell you, in many of the conversations, sex seems always to be the number one issue. (See Chapter 15 for more on this.) One thing is for sure, when it comes to sex, women are consistent. If a woman loves having sex with her man, she's going to be the same after they get married. If she didn't like it before, giving her a ring is not going to change things. Sex definitely has its place, but it doesn't guarantee fidelity. Being married to a pro-athlete, I was exposed to a lot of useful information about men. Men would say, plain and clear, "Even if I was married to Halle Berry I would cheat." These are the same men who left their wives and kids for the same groupies who left them as soon as the money stopped flowing in. I must admit sex was *never* an issue in my marriage, yet I still came across florist receipts, letters that said, "I love you. Wish I could be with you," (and they weren't addressed to me), naked pictures sent to his cell phone, online chats with unsuspecting girlfriends, and all the rest. As a married woman with a husband who cheated, I've been through it, too. I too have walked in those shoes. Yet, at the end of the day, I said "I do" to Cory Hall. And he is the only one I can rightfully be mad at, not the other woman. To take it a step further, I should only be mad at myself. A person can only do to you what you allow him or her to do. Ladies, we have to take responsibility for what we accept. The blame cannot be placed on anyone but ourselves. Fool me once, shame on you. Fool me twice, shame on me.

Now let me make this clear, I don't condone women dating married men but the sentiment has nothing to do with the man's wife. It is because I think it's a waste of time and time is something that not even all the money in the world can replace. Most women I know, who have dated married men, end up very hurt and emotionally distraught.

A married man can only do two things for you, have sex with you and pay you. Anything else is on borrowed time. When the weekend or evening is over or when holidays come, he's going home to his family. Why waste time on a married man when you can spend that time looking for and dating someone single?

Never date a married man with the mindset that one day he will leave his wife. If he does leave his wife, in time he will probably leave you, too. If you feel yourself falling in love with a married man, stop while you're ahead (or behind). He is not going to leave his wife (generally speaking). Statistics say that there is only a 3 percent chance that a married man will leave his wife for the other woman, so unless you are really lucky or the timing is just right, the odds are against you, And remember, often what's done in the dark does come to light. You can bank on the fact that when the man's wife finds out, the great majority of men will break it off with the other woman without any hesitation and will act like she was never alive.

Ladies, if you are going to date a married man, make sure the benefits outweigh the losses. Be aware of what you are getting yourself into. Know the rules and don't try to bend them. If you don't know them, here they are:

- Don't be delusional and think that you are the only one, especially if he's rich. A man's options are as long as his money.
- You can't treat a married man like "your man" cause he ain't.
- Stop while you're ahead.

A married male friend once told me, "Shanae, There's no reason to date at all if the man you're talking to doesn't add something to your life. If you are dating a married man, or any man for that matter, make sure you can get some bills paid off!" He must have been reading my mind.

Affairs are like a seventh day. They are a break from all duties and obligations and responsibilities. I'm not saying this is right and I'm not saying it lightly. This is just how they are. You can't be responsible when you're with your lover. And since you already know you're way out of line, you go the extra distance. You throw yourself in headfirst. You become the very personification of irresponsible. You are way alive. Every detail sings. It would be a great way to live if it weren't so ruinous.
—Wendy Plump

Rhonda

Being involved with someone who is legally married to someone else or in a live-in situation is a waste of time and energy, yet it happens every day. I have done it and it was hurtful and futile. However, I must point out the obvious: The "other woman" can't wreck a home or steal a married man. A woman cannot make a guy cheat or not cheat. A man decides what he is going to do and what he is willing to risk from the beginning, and the other woman decides to accept less than a full relationship from the beginning. We don't always know why these situations occur. Perhaps the marriage was already "wrecked" or things were already breaking down and no one was talking about it—or maybe it was just "fine" and a situation was presented that allowed the cheating to occur. The bottom line is such choices are made by two adults and the consequences must be mutually owned. If you are or have been involved in a relationship with a married man or have been on the other side of that situation, it's up to you to decide where to go from here.

Married men are everywhere. They are in grocery stores, nightclubs, strip clubs, corporate offices, and on dating websites hiding behind exotic Internet usernames. For the record, I have had several relationships with married men. They are usually in some sort of delusional state about their marital status and out telling heartfelt stories about why they are "in search of" someone else—some with real issues others not so much. The stories range from "I haven't had sex in years," "She has really let herself go over time" to "We don't have anything in common; I love going to the beach, she hates it. I love to go out and shoot pool, and she wants to visit her girlfriends instead." Then there are the classics like "I love her, but I am not in love with her," or "I stay because of the kids. I couldn't imagine not being around my children." I think I have heard them all. Maybe you have heard a few, too. It would be almost comical if it wasn't so outrageous, asinine, and sad.

Married men are often looking to prey on single women. The other day, I was browsing a popular dating site and noticed a unique message for me from a user ID I did not recognize. I clicked on the picture and before I could read the message, I realized that I had met this guy in an Atlanta restaurant about four months earlier with my girlfriend.

During our initial meeting, he introduced himself to me and struck up a conversation about his business. He made small talk and presented himself both respectfully and professionally. He offered to buy me a drink and we continued talking. During our conversation, he mentioned that he had recently married the "woman of his dreams." He also was a self-admitted "player" prior to marriage. He explained that he used Internet dating sites as a way to keep four or five women on his sex/date list at all times. "As a single man, I ran the streets and frequented nightclubs for ten years straight, that is until I met "Ms. Right," he also admitted. She was the one who was worthy of the ring and getting his last name. I told him I thought it was great he found "her," and we continued talking until I finished my drink. He then walked me to my car. I never gave that night nor him a second thought until I saw his picture on the dating site.

There he was, Mr. *"happily married,"* Mr. *"I married the woman of my dreams,"* on the singles dating site, hiding behind an exotic login ID! Although his message read, "You are beautiful. I am interested in you," he didn't realize he had met me four months prior and told me his wonderful love story! I responded to the e-mail message, "You ought to be ashamed of yourself. I believe we met a few months ago or do you have a twin?" He was online when I responded and within seconds, acknowledged he remembered me, and asked me to call him. He put his number in the reply message and wrote, "Please call me." I didn't respond.

Just think, if I would have never met him and didn't know his story, I might have gone on a date with him. I would have been an innocent bystander accused of being a home wrecker.

We must understand that none of us can make a man, much less a married man, start or stop anything, no matter how good we are in the bedroom, the boardroom, or the kitchen. He has to want to start or stop it. Period. I learned this very early on the hard way. We woman must start looking at this from a broader perspective.

Now let's go back to my indiscretions. My love life has been filled with all the passion, excitement, and all the drama I could generate and manage. It was clear that while I was seeking to fill a void within myself, I was on a self-destructive path. In the end, this path proved to be selfish and was extremely damaging to all involved—the wives and all of our kids. Although they approached, pursued, wooed, and entertained me, when it was all said and done, and the secret revealed, I was the one who was left holding the bag. I was still single and they went back to their wives.

Married men still approach me and my single girlfriends and probably some of you, too. We run into them at the sports bar, jazz concerts, grocery stores, casinos, the gym, and a host of other places. They seem more prevalent and bold today than they were in my younger days. Yet, I still can't help but wonder *why?* Why aren't they at home pursuing the women to whom they gave their vows and pledged faithfulness? Why are they on the streets? And how do they have time to juggle a relationship with another woman?

Many would say, "They are just being true to themselves," "They are hunters," and "They are just being men." However, the point is, as women, we have to see the situation exactly for what it is. In other words, we have to personally acknowledge what's going on without any delusion well before deciding on the course of action we will take, and where necessary, we have to take responsibility for what we accept and our role in the demise, if any.

About three years ago, I met a man at a happy-hour gathering at an old-school, hole-in-the-wall restaurant in South Atlanta. My girlfriend asked me to meet her there after work. She said they had good food, good drinks, and great music—all of which sounded great even though that area of town wasn't really my preference. Since she arrived before me, she saved me a seat. Apparently, Friday nights were a popular night. But before I could get there, she called me on the phone and said, "Hey, how far are you? I met this older gentleman who seems nice. He's leaving, but I told him he had to meet you first." When I got there, I spotted her at the bar talking to someone. I assumed it must be the guy. I saw her point me out to him and immediately his face lit up with a huge smile. When I got to where they were, he extended his hand and politely told me his name. We will call him *Mr. MF*. He then went on to say,"I was about to leave, but I ain't going nowhere now. I see why your friend wanted me to meet you. Let's party and have some fun!"

Mr. MF bought our drinks and food. He shared that he was a small business owner and had a contract in Atlanta, but that his home was in another southern state. As if he had to prove his success, he then took out his phone to show me a photo of a luxurious home and a black Corvette. He said he owned them both. "I sure would like to take you for a ride in my car. A red bone in a black Corvette is sexy," he said. He told me he was single and looking for his "queen." No ring on his finger. Not even a ring line. While he was no Denzel, or Brad Pitt, I thought he was nice, kind, laid back, and funny. He didn't dress to impress, and he wasn't the type of guy I would normally pick. He looked like he could have been fifty-something. He was slightly bald, with graying hair and a medium-sized round stomach. He had strong-looking arms with big hands and feet, and his teeth were in need of some dental work. Yet, he had a lot of confidence and was a real gentleman. *Swagger,* if you will. It was in his mannerisms, his walk and talk. We danced, talked, and exchanged numbers. He was fun. At the end of the night, I thought I liked him. He was older and seemed settled. He walked us to our cars and we all went our separate ways.

The months that followed proved to be eye-opening and a life-changing experience. Mr. MF and I began casually dating shortly after our meeting. Prior to our first date, we talked on the phone a couple of times. During these conversations, he reiterated that he was single, assured me he could take care of me financially, and let me know that he was very attracted to me and wanted to date me.

One Sunday afternoon he called and I missed the call. Within minutes, I called him back. He didn't answer, so I left a message. I didn't hear from him 'til early the next morning on his way to work. Clue number one?

I wasn't really looking for anything serious, just someone to go to the movies with, have occasional dinners with, and do normal dating things. I still had a ton of baggage from my divorce, and I was in the process of trying to find myself again.

Since I liked that Mr. MF was ten years my senior and seemed stable and settled, I was willing to put aside some of the "superficial" things that I usually looked for in men (the corporate look, nice body, great shoes, fine clothes, great teeth . . . you get the idea). I was willing to go with him based on how he treated me. We began dining out, took a trip to a casino, went to a concert, and had weekly crab and dance nights together. I liked the get-up-and-go in him. He was spontaneous and liked to do stuff and, more importantly, he wanted me with him. I also loved that he was a hard worker and could afford anything we did without hesitation. Eventually, he revealed to me that he had been making a high six-figure income for years and over the past three years he had been making seven figures (which explained his swagger). He then said he wanted to put me on his "payroll," so I could always have spending money. I liked the sound of that. He also started giving me very generous monthly gifts and began making sure my bills were paid. Three months came and went rather quickly. I was enjoying my time with Mr. MF.

Then, one day, out of nowhere, I received a text message that read, "You can believe there is a Mrs. MF out here." I forwarded the text to Mr. MF and asked him who wrote it and what did it all mean. He called immediately and said, "That's just a woman who won't let go. We broke up and she's still hanging on and trying to mess things up for me." I said, "Oh, okay" and we kept dating.

During the course of our relationship, there were times when he had to go back to his home state. After all, he was running two very successful businesses so I never second-guessed those trips. I had no reason not to believe him. The way I saw it, "What married man could be away from home for weeks at a time, spend weekends out, generously spend money, and go to dinner at will"?

Weeks passed and I received yet another text message stating again that Mr. MF was married. I responded by asking the person to call me so I could get to the bottom of the situation. She didn't call. I later learned, through a series of text messages from Mr. MF's wife, that he was indeed married. Although we never talked by the phone, she would text me whenever she felt the urge.

I confronted Mr. MF on several occasions after these texts, and he finally admitted that he was married. I was angered beyond words. By this time, I was emotionally involved and financially dependent on him. For the first time, I didn't have to be "Ms. Independent," or be concerned with how something was going to be paid. I was focused on me. I was working out daily, reading more, and taking care of my children and my very ill dad without having to worry about anything. Now this. We went round and round about the lies, the marital status, the chaos, and the drama. He lied and lied. He denied loving her and denied they slept together. Now every time he went back to his home state, I knew he was really at "home" with his wife. I called off our relationship several times, for months at a time. I began to look for ways to generate more business with my company, and I started to apply for other work. I needed to wean myself from him and my financial dependence on him.

Several times he called and said, "Let me take you to dinner. I have something to show you." I eventually agreed, and we met at one of our favorite restaurants. While at dinner, he presented me with a court document that showed he had filed for divorce. He said, "I know what I can live with, but more importantly, I know what I can't live without. Rhonda, I don't want to live without you. I don't care how much it costs me to get a divorce, I want you to be in my life for the rest of my life."

I started dating him again, feeling that he must be sincere and really care about me if he has filed for divorce. He continued to go home for work and claimed that he was staying at his parents' house during the divorce. Almost six months passed, and I heard nothing more about the divorce or the divorce proceedings. I didn't ask. He didn't tell. We kept dating, until one day I asked about the status of the divorce. The look on his face told me everything. The responses didn't make sense. The lies poured out. I knew then that neither he nor the situation was going to change, so I had to change.

Needless to say, he never got a divorce. I began to see him merely as a friend. A friend whose good deeds still allowed him into my space but whose lies tore at the core of my belief system about men and relationships. His contract in Atlanta unexpectedly expired and he eventually moved back to his hometown. But for years that followed he made my life easier from a financial standpoint. Why? You ask. Maybe he feels guilty, I don't really know. To this day, I am in awe at the degree to which he lied to bring me into his life and keep me there.

It is surreal. Had someone told me that a man, over 55, would or could lie so much to have another woman in his life, I would have never believed them. In the end, I didn't get mad. I got real. What doesn't kill you only makes you stronger.

Dating a married man is usually lose-lose. Even if you win financially, you still lose. This type of relationship is not long term. It merely satisfies immediate or short-term needs, while preventing you from finding something more permanent. My story isn't yours. Perhaps you have or can find a fulfilling relationship with a married man that completes you. If so, you have to take that journey. These stories are out there, and they are real. It's up to us to learn what to do and not do and how to deal with the men in our lives. Say what you will, but don't hate the player, hate the game. And if you must blame, start at home with the person standing in the mirror looking at you.

Chapter 3
The Single Guy

Rhonda

Ahhh, the single man. What does that really mean? There are married men who say, "I am single." There are legally single men in committed relationships who say, "I am single." There are also "single men" who are really living alone and single by all standards. I'd like to give a shout out to the "real" single men! While most women have experienced each of the types of "single men" described, this chapter is about the "unmarried, single man who lives alone." This chapter is brief. If a guy is truly single, there isn't much to say. Yet, be aware that *single* doesn't always mean *sincere*. Before all of you women shout *Hallelujah* at a man truly being single, or the one who says he is single, remember that being single offers no guarantees. You just get to skip the drama of dealing with another woman. That's all. No more. No less.

I've been divorced since 2004. Months after leaving my husband, I decided that I would not only find dates the traditional way—at the office, the store, restaurants, or other places—but that I would also try online dating. So, I created a profile on one of the more popular African

American dating sites. I also created a Facebook page. Not only did my dating options increase a hundred fold, but so did the drama that comes with the highs and lows of dating after forty!

Every day, I would get lists of possible dates from the online dating site. The list was so long that I could go out on a date almost every other day if I accepted the invitation of each potential suitor. Girlfriend, this type of dating makes you feel like a star. It seems like everybody wants you. The screening process, however, reduces those numbers to double digits, then to single digits, after a few conversations or e-mails.

One day, after more than a month of e-mailing and talking to a handsome fifty-year-old bachelor with a military background and a prominent position in his home state of Alabama, I took him up on his offer for a dinner date. He then planned a trip to Atlanta the upcoming weekend. Although his profile said "not looking for a relationship of any kind" and "just chilling and having fun," I figured once he saw me in all my "loveliness," he would want a relationship.

I loved talking to him on the phone. He was smart, grown, established, old-fashioned in some ways, witty, engaging, and verbally affectionate. He called morning, noon, and night, on breaks, and in the wee hours of the morning when he couldn't sleep. "Hi, baby girl," he would say, or

"Hi, doll," and then the conversation would just take off in all directions. We talked about everything from kids to jobs, life, aging, music, and relationships. We also talked about our past marriages. It was open, fun, and fulfilling.

As if to mesmerize me with his words, he warned in the most gentle and soft-spoken voice, "You will love me; you won't be able to help it. I am a gentleman. I present myself well. I will give you my undivided attention on every date. I'm affectionate. I will treat you well because I understand women. But remember, I am not looking for anything. I like being single." This was all new to me so I didn't pay much attention to his words.

We went on our first date, at a very nice restaurant, and the conversation was great. He was just as funny in person as he was on the phone. He made jokes about me being late to dinner, and we talked as though we were old friends. More handsome in person than in his pictures, he dressed with style—nice slacks, great shoes, a stylish hat, and he smelled amazing. Towering at six foot one, he was physically fit and had beautiful white teeth to go along with his smooth, caramel skin. A perfect gentleman he was indeed. After dinner he walked me to my car, and while holding my hand, opened my car door, put me in, and gave me a quick kiss on the lips. He thanked me for being his date and told me he wanted to see me again. I thought, *Thank you God! My knight in shining armor has indeed arrived!*

We talked often over the next month. Then he came to town to visit me and take me on another date. This time we met at the Georgia Aquarium; we held hands, walked, ate lunch, and talked for hours. He was incredibly attentive and sweet. We parted and agreed to meet later that evening. That night, I met him at his hotel and got into his car to head out for the night. I was late and we were both hungry. He took me to a great lounge type restaurant, a place near the area he was staying. The dinner was superb and he duplicated everything he did on date number one and more. This time he sat next to me at dinner instead of across from me. He continuously kissed my hand at the table and looked me in my eyes as I talked to him. Becoming even more comfortable, he gently draped his arm on the back of our booth. We had a few drinks. I had a couple of margaritas, and he had a few Long Island iced teas. We were having a great time. The energy was amazing.

The restaurant's ambiance, the chemistry between us, and the comfortableness we shared with each other made it impossible to leave this man. Yes, I knew it was "going down" on date number two. After several hours of enjoying the band, each other's conversation, and our drinks, we went back to his hotel and had a great time.

The next day, we talked three or four times throughout the day. We spoke warmly about the date, while joking about different aspects of it. I didn't call him; he always called me. It was safer for me that way. Clearly, he must have had feelings for me.

Several more weeks went by and we went on another date. This time we went to a local sports bar to watch the Final Four games. I love sports. We didn't stay out too long. He had a six o'clock wake-up call for work. And instead of him staying at a hotel, I invited him to stay with me. I had the house to myself that weekend. This time we made what I would call "love." Afterward, we cuddled, talked, and enjoyed our time together. It felt so "normal" To have him in my room in my house. He got up very early the next day, kissed me goodbye, and went to work.

Ironically, after this visit, our conversations became less frequent. Instead of four to five calls a day, it was more like two to three. I had more feelings for him and he was calling less. During some of our talks, he would gently say, "Look at you, willing to give your heart to me. Baby girl, you gotta be careful. You are too sweet and too precious. You gotta learn to protect your heart." I disregarded every one of his comments. I let my emotions get the best of me, and I let him know that I really liked him. I didn't know what to make of the constant calls, and the sweet conversations at all times of the day and night. Yet, our relationship wasn't growing. I didn't know what to think.

Disregarding his initial warnings, I still proceed as I would with any other man who I believed was genuinely interested. I will never forget one day when I was on my way to Los Angeles for a quick getaway to see my daughter. He and I had just spoken while I was driving to the airport. He called, like he often did, and told me that he would be out of the country for several weeks for work and asked what I was up to. I told him I was traveling to Los Angeles. He seemed mildly upset and said, "You're always going somewhere; stop being so fast." I took his comments lightly. We laughed and chatted some and then he wished me a safe trip.

Just before taking off, I made my final calls and sent my texts to loved ones to let them know that I loved them and that I was on my way to Los Angeles—a practice I do before every flight, just in case. On this trip, however, I also sent Mr. Alabama a text and for the first time, I said, "I want you to know that I love you. I need you to know this, just in case something happens on this flight." Then I turned off my phone and endured my four-hour flight. I couldn't wait to land, not only because I missed my daughter, but I couldn't wait to turn on my phone and see what he said in return.

When I arrived in Los Angeles, I turned on my phone—and guess what? I had messages, but not one damn response from my knight in shining armor! Not one! I could confirm he received the message because I set my phone up to show when messages have been read (y'all know what I am talking about). I have to be honest, I was a little disappointed. No, I was *a lot* disappointed. Surely he felt something close to what I felt, right?

Okay, so the next day I was getting dressed to go out when Mr. Alabama called me (mind you, he was out of the country). We are chopping it up like we always do and somehow we get on the topic of love and somewhere in that discussion he says, "Baby girl, it's not like that for me." With my self-esteem in pieces and my mouth slightly stuck in the open position (like "Oh, My God"), somehow I muster up some discombobulated conversation, a little laughter, and then told him that I was headed out "to make it do what it do." We closed out the call cordially and I went out.

Do you see any red flags or confusing messages? Although I had read many relationship books including Steve Harvey's, *Act Like a Lady, Think Like a Man,* I fell for someone who clearly stated, in the beginning, that he didn't want a relationship! He maintained his "single and loving it" position, even though he was very attentive and warm toward me. Yet, I didn't want to see the signs on the wall. This goes back to Chapter 1, "You Can't Change Him." Both people have to have their minds and hearts in the same place to consummate a mutually exclusive relationship.

So much for Mr. Alabama; back to Facebook. Just as I completed my Facebook page, I got a "friend" request from an old college boyfriend from California. I will call him LT. I couldn't believe my eyes! My bodybuilding cutie pie still looked great! He told me he had "been looking for me for over twenty years." I was ecstatic. I needed a distraction from the confusion. He asked for my e-mail address and telephone number, and I gave them to him. Later that evening, he called.

Although Mr. Alabama and I continued to talk from time to time, I began talking to and eventually going to see my old college sweetheart. Mr. Alabama seemed a little taken aback when he found out I was talking to someone else. "I didn't know you were going to start dating so soon," he said, in a very gentle voice. "You are moving too fast, baby girl." Excuse me? I wasn't moving too fast. I was getting over one man with another. It felt nice to be wanted.

LT was dark chocolate, five foot ten, forty-six years old, and funny. His smile was killer. Skin smooth as silk. His body was better than I remembered. When LT and I first began talking, I made it clear that I didn't pay for trips to see a man. If he wanted to begin seeing me, he would have to make it possible given we lived on two different coasts. LT sent for me several times over the next few months, including a trip to Vegas.

On a visit to Sacramento, my hometown, LT took me down memory lane. He kissed my hand while he drove me to the college where we met. He hugged me in front of the school hall where he used to carry my books to class. He looked in my eyes and reminisced about details that even I had forgotten. He drove me to the home that I had lived in with my mom—I would have never been able to find that house! When we pulled up, I think I saw tears in his eyes. He drove me by his old apartment where we spent many fun days and nights. In my mind, I hoped I could get over Alabama and engage in the romantic story that was evolving between LT and me. LT suggested that I write about it after the wedding. Yes, I said wedding. He had asked my ring size, told me, "I am never letting you go this time." Talk about being overwhelmed! For several months, we spent quality time together. He massaged my feet as I watched television. He held me, talked to me, and made me laugh. He was fun and sexy.

LT lived alone in a home he had owned for many years, drove a nice BMW, and he gave me his undivided attention. By week three, LT was saying, "I love you, Rhonda. I always have." And every text and phone call ended with "I love you." I told my friends and family about how we became reacquainted and how happy I was to be back in his life. He put it on Facebook for all his friends and family to see. I lived in Georgia and he lived in California, but I was willing to try a long-distance relationship with LT. I had forgotten why we broke up years ago. Although I felt something wasn't quite right about him, the distance would give me time to examine what I really wanted and needed in a man.

One weekend Alabama called and asked what I was doing. After telling him my plans for the evening, I asked him when he was coming back to Atlanta. He said, “I am headed there now. I’ll be crossing over the state line in about twenty minutes.” Butterflies began floating in my stomach and my hands became sweaty. I then said, “Why didn’t you tell me you were coming to town?” I listened, waiting. Finally, “Baby girl, the way you have been traveling, I just thought you might be on a flight somewhere,” he said. We laughed and talked a bit more. Then he told me that he had to meet a few guys from his military unit and inquired if he could see me later.

Have you ever had that weird feeling in your stomach when you know you are about to do some crazy shit—something that won’t make much sense the next day? “Well, if time permits, before I have to meet my girlfriend,” is what I finally said. My hair wasn’t done, and I had no idea what I would wear. He called about two hours later. The first time, I let the call go to voicemail. The second time I answered. He was at the sports bar where we had watched the college games. He was in my neighborhood!

I told him that I would meet him there, but I wouldn’t stay long because I was meeting my girlfriend. He said, “We could just grab a bite to eat and you can carry on with your plans.” I got dressed and headed out. Driving over there my head was spinning and my heart was skipping a beat. I was excited about seeing Mr. Alabama.

I walked into the bar and our eyes met. He gave me a warm hug and a quick kiss. We sat across from each other. And within seconds he came and sat next to me. He was in a Polo pullover, some jeans, and the perfect loafers. Plus, he was smelling good as usual. We ordered our food and began small talk when my phone began ringing. It was my girlfriend. I didn't answer. She sent a text: "How long before you get to the spot?" I didn't respond. She called again and again. I received several other calls. I didn't answer. If Jesus himself had called, I don't know if I would have answered! Okay, maybe if Jesus called I would have answered, but it would have been a quick talk!

We finished dinner an hour and a half later. He walked me to my car and we reluctantly said goodbye. I called my girlfriend when I got in the car to ask where she was. She said, "Girl, I'm back home." I made up some story about why I didn't get her calls or texts, and apologized. I immediately called Mr. Alabama. He was headed back to his hotel. He asked if I was still going out, I told him unfortunately not because my girlfriend had gone back home. He suggested we meet at a lounge, have a drink, and talk some more. I agreed. We had a great night together, and then I went home and went to sleep in my own bed.

The next day I noticed I was missing the necklace I had been wearing the night before. I sent a text message and asked him to look for it. I told him what a great time I had and how nice it was to see him. Moments later, I got a text that read, “No necklace found.” That was it! “No necklace found.” I responded, “Thanks. Yes, I made it home safe. Yes, I am okay, and yes, it was good to see you, too.”

Moments later the phone rang. “Sorry doll, I should have made sure you were okay,” he said. I didn’t hear from him again for over two weeks. I sent a text to see how he was doing. No response. A day or so later, I sent another one. No response. WTF? Didn’t he feel all that amazing energy we shared just weeks prior? Eventually, I heard from him. He said he had had a “family emergency.” Yeah, right and I am the tooth fairy!

He started calling again. I began to ignore his calls. After I didn’t answer a few times, he got the message. It was clear that I liked him and I believe he liked me as well, but I also realized that this relationship was at a standstill. It was never going to go to the next level no matter how many sweet talks we shared or *baby girls* he called me. I took my power back. Today, we still talk on occasions but I hold my ground.

Trying to reconnect, LT and I began to talk on the phone again. We never discussed monogamy per se, but we did talk about a future together. Yet, something had changed. He was still verbally affectionate but still something felt different. Then one Friday night, while I was out with some friends, I received a text message that he had purchased a ticket for me to come to Sacramento. I had mixed feelings about the trip, but I decided to accept his invitation.

That same night while I lay sleeping, I received two calls from an unknown caller, back to back. When I woke up the next morning, I saw the missed calls and listened to the messages. It was a woman who identified herself as "LT's ex-girlfriend, Linda." "LT ain't the man you think he is," the female voice said. "He's a liar, a cheater, and he's been begging me to come back to him for the past month." As if that were not enough information, in the second message she left her phone number and asked me to please call her. "Listen, I know you know him from college," she continued, "He's told me all about you over the past five years. LT is not the same guy you knew in college. Please call me so we can talk. I have e-mails and text messages to prove everything. He has been begging me to come back to him also." Then she hung up the phone.

I was surprised, shocked, and disgusted all in the same breath. Do single, college sweethearts hunt you down for twenty years, fly you out to see them, take you shopping, drive you down memory lane, say all the right words, massage your feet, tell you they love you and want to marry you, and take you to Vegas only to make their ex-girlfriends jealous enough to want them back?
Do they? Yes, they do.

I called Linda back. She talked and I listened. I asked for proof of what she was saying. She forwarded me numerous e-mails and text messages he had sent her over the past few months. Some of them read, "I love you, you are the only woman for me." "I want to marry you, please call me." Others were, "No one can ever take your place, I love everything about you." And, "I miss you so much, please come back." They were all sent on different dates, at different times, but during the same time he was showering me with so much attention. Now, I was smart enough to know to take everything with a grain of salt because I had been in Linda's shoes before. I've called the other woman to tell her the "truth" so that I could "protect" her from the pain and lies, and all that other stuff. Yet, some of this was indisputable. I was perplexed. What did all this mean?

I wasn't angry. I was surprised and caught off guard. I had been here before. It was quite familiar. I knew the drama all too well. I knew the break up, the make up, the in-between relationships, the fear of letting go, the fear of someone else getting "my man," and the ego-based holding on. Yep. Been there, done that. I called LT and shared with him what I had learned. Of course he denied it and called her the infamous "crazy" and said she was just trying to mess things up for him. *I have heard that somewhere before,* but I digress yet again. When it was all said and done, I told my old college friend that it appears he had some unfinished business with his "ex"-girlfriend. I bid them both good luck and went on about my life. Both Alabama and LT were amazing parts of my journey toward understanding single men and myself.

Lesson Learned from Mr. Alabama

When a single guy says, "I am not looking for a relationship. I like being single," believe him! Appreciate him for his courage and realness. This type of single guy is a rare commodity. If you choose to continue to date him and it does not materialize into love, even after your sexiness, beauty, long talks, great laughs, wonderful dinners, and love-making, you cannot be mad at him. He was honest. But remember, if he likes you at all, he will continue to partake of the goodies as often as you let him. He will continue to call and hang around as long as the situation works for him. If he doesn't like you or isn't attracted to you, you won't have this problem. He will be long gone after he gets the goodies the first time. Shout out to Mr. Alabama! I love that guy.

Lesson Learned from LT, My College Sweetheart

Even when a single guy lives alone, says and does all the right things, takes you shopping, makes you laugh, kisses your hand while driving, tells everyone in his circle that he found you again, and tells you he loves you and promises to marry you, there are still no guarantees about his faithfulness and who holds his heart. So be patient, be careful, and make sure you get what you want and need out of the situation. Even if the old girlfriend comes back, you can move on, knowing that you gained something—besides another lesson. LT and I remain friends but it was a situation best left in the past. What I learned from all of this was that I needed to slow down.

Remember, single means there is room for you, but sometimes the wall around a man's heart is too thick to penetrate. We have to ask the same questions about men that they ask about us. Why are you single if you have all these great qualities? Sometimes they are hiding secrets or haven't told you the whole story. Dating is all fun and games (meaning no real expectations) until you are both committed and married. If you have a man that you like, enjoy what you have with him when you are together and take your time before escalating your feelings and the relationship to the next level. It all must be mutual in order for it to work.

Chapter 4

The Man Looking for Love

This man is a rare commodity. The disturbing thing for the man who wrote the letter that follows is that women have been put through so much foolishness that it's hard to decipher between the jackass and the man who genuinely wants love. But if I had to show you a letter from a man looking for love, this would be it.

Love Letter to Rhonda

Rhonda, thank you for sharing your thoughts and feelings with me today. You are a beautiful woman with a wonderful spirit. I'm very happy that you're comfortable enough with me to share some of your personal thoughts, experiences, and emotions. That means more to me than words could ever express. You're something very special, Rhonda—a gift. I felt something unique about you when I first saw the flash of your precious smile and the gleam in your eyes. Your pictures portray the warmth and gentleness that is reflected in your letter to me. Meeting you is no accident. I am certain that our meeting was predetermined by a higher power to let us both know that we can find our heart's desire again, if we are patient. You are the essence of what I want in my life as my friend, lover, and partner. What I feel in my heart toward you is not a crush nor an infatuation. It is a genuine admiration for your style, grace, and personality. Please don't misunderstand what I'm saying to you. I realize we just met and there is soooo much we have to learn about each other. But, you have my full, undivided attention. I'm very poised, very patient, and understanding. Rhonda, I know an angel with only one wing, with a song in his heart he has yet to sing. He wanders without aim between earth and sky, searching for his soulmate to help him fly. He asked the Lord one lonely night, "With only one wing, Lord, will I ever take flight?" The Lord then answered in his mysterious way, "The wing you are missing will find you one day. I created my angels with only one wing, each one a king in search of his queen. When you see her, then you'll know why. She too is without aim between earth and sky. Until that time, angel, don't lose sight. Your missing wing is searching tonight. And when she finds you, then you'll finally see, that your wings joined together will set you free." I have been waiting for my missing wing and I may have found her. Seeing and meeting you on this site some time ago, then canceling my membership approximately the same time you did, then coming back within literally days of you rejoining is no accident. I am certain that our meeting was predetermined by a higher power. However, I will reluctantly fade away into the background if you're not interested in pursuing something serious with me. And I will always wonder, "Are you my other wing?" And what a life with you would have been like. Will I ever know? I hope so.

Very truly yours,

Nathaniel

Rhonda

Wow, what a letter! First and foremost, I discovered through the editing process that the "wing" portion of this lovely letter was from a poem written by *RosesAreBlue* so we want to ensure they get proper credit for their poetry. I guess we have to start "Google-ing" our love letters now to make sure they are authentic works. Wow! On to the point, there is something to be said about a man who can put a love letter together. But there is more to be said about a woman who can see past the words and get to the heart of the man writing it. I loved Nathaniel's letter. It was very touching, but something made me question his sincerity. Intuitively, I felt I needed to pay close attention.

Nathaniel's Internet picture revealed a handsome man, in his mid-forties, probably six foot four or so; brown skin, nice teeth, muscular, large frame, nice wavy salt and pepper hair, and a friendly smile. He photographed himself. He was seated in a Hummer, a fitting vehicle for someone his size. We had many long conversations. We talked about me caring for my dad, who was suffering from Alzheimer's, and he thought I was quite compassionate. We also talked about our children, our jobs, our desires, and our goals. He informed me that he owned a successful business, that he was settled, and that he was looking for a wife who he could love. Our conversations were more of the usual getting to know someone chatter.

After the third week of talking on the phone and e-mailing back and forth, my new friend said to me, "Rhonda, I feel like I have known you forever. We have this energy and connection that is unreal. I believe I have found my soulmate. I want you to think about moving to Seattle. You can bring your dad and your kids. I will take care of all of you and we can have a good life together. Baby, but first, come and visit me and let's take in the upcoming festivals and this beautiful weather we are having here. We will just hang out, and then we can talk about my moving you to Seattle."

I was excited to meet him and to go to Seattle because I had never been there. I told him that I wanted to bring a girlfriend along on this first trip for safety reasons, he said, "Great, I will have you both sitting in first class and sipping Mimosas on your way." I advised him that I would need a room and that I would rent my own car to be able to get around freely. "No problem, baby" he said. "I will buy your tickets next Friday."

A few days after this conversation, he called and said, "Rhonda, I would like to spend time with you alone before your friend comes and I would prefer you stay at my home. My house is big enough for all of us to stay comfortably," to which I replied, "No, I am not comfortable with that, I must have my own room" and although I don't normally bring friends along on dates, this was different, I had never met him, he lived in another state, and my background in correctional work made me suspicious. In order to work with him, I told him it would be okay to send for my friend later that day, to allow a few hours alone to talk but that she had to come as well. Call it what you want, I was being safe. He said, "No problem, baby, I will get the tickets Friday."

The day before Nathaniel was to buy the tickets for the trip, I received a text saying, "I have an emergency meeting in San Francisco for my company. I will have to reschedule your visit." Not a call, a text. I was not surprised. Long story short, I never met my Seattle-based friend in person. Now thinking about him and the charming words he spoke, his gentleness and kindness, I could have seen myself introducing my kids to him. He was a father, seemed to have all the good qualities I liked, and had shown me enough to make me consider dating him.

Not to switch subjects, ladies, but I have to tie this point in here.

How many times have you met a guy and thought he could be the "one" or at least you thought he is someone you want to know better? Now in how many situations like that have you decided to introduce him to your kids based on the talks, feelings, and emotions? Probably many. Had this guy been closer to where I lived, the odds are, I would have begun dating him and introduced him to my family. If we follow the advice of Mr. Harvey, who suggests we introduce our kids to men we are dating, before you finish the deal, we might be introducing them more often than not. I get this point to a degree but I will tell you from experience, it just isn't healthy for the kids. If you ask any of my daughters how they felt about meeting guys who I thought cared about me, only to find them missing down the road, they will tell you they hated it and that it was confusing. This applies to many platonic male friends as well.

Your children may not mind meeting your friends John, Tom, and Steve, then being left to wonder why they haven't come by in a while, but I will tell you, mine did. Having learned the hard way, Shanae has taken a different approach. She opts not to have men meet my grandchildren. We have to make careful decisions for the sake of our children. If you decide to have them meet, after he has proven himself to you and you have checked him out through and through, then have a talk with the kids and let them know they will be meeting someone very special, your friend so and so. Then plan for a get together in a family friendly arena, like a park or skating rink. Once you introduce them, watch how he interacts, is he stiff and fake or genuine and relaxed? Listen to their responses and watch body language and keep it real about your parenting style, your expectations, and your hopes and dreams when it comes to talking about your role as a mom. Remember not every guy you meet deserves to meet your kids or your family. Choose wisely. You don't want to be like the girl that cried wolf, telling your kids and family every other month that you have met the "one." Eventually they won't believe you anymore and won't trust your judgment.

Now back to Mr. Seattle. After the trip cancellation, he apologized, continued to send sweet e-mails and texts. He also continued to call from time to time with lengthy conversations filled with sweet talk (aka bull crap). Yet, I began to see through him. I asked enough of the right questions, and he began to get his stories mixed up. We never made it on a date, but the letter was so beautifully written and the incident so poignant, that I had to share it so you could be aware of how powerful and deep the deception can be in a single woman's world. With each conversation, I began to pay more attention to the details. I got past the "fluff" and began to notice the inconsistencies in his stories. I finally called it like it was and sent him on his poetic way. I can't help but wonder how many women he has mesmerized on the Internet with this same letter?

About a month later, I received a friend request from him on Facebook. WTF?

All jokes aside, ladies, there is no greater feeling on planet earth than love. We all want it, and we all have it in us to give. It is a gift to be cherished, to share, and to be thankful for every day. The sad part is, when we want it so bad that we fall for the mere words from a guy who is really a poet, player, or pimp. If they sound good enough and we are lonely enough, the words that sound like love get us excited and make us lose our footing, even when we haven't seen any actions to support them. Proceed with caution.

Take care of your heart. Honor your inner voice and notice signs written on the wall because they may be trying to tell you something. I can say that I have had the blessing of having men love me a few times in my life and the thing that is consistent is that real love is genuine. It will seem as if the man really does eat and breathe you. Not in the crazy stalker kind of way, but in a calm, sweet, and vulnerable way. My ex-husband is one of those persons.

I can remember a time when he had gone to Las Vegas for a convention. He called often to let me know he was thinking of me and missed me. He had a paid hotel room at one of the casinos. Yet, while we were talking on the phone, he decided right in the middle of our conversation that he was going to drive all the way back home just to be next to me that night. It was a seven-hour drive.
We both talked to each other with such excitement and anticipation. He didn't care how tired he was, or that he could have been resting or playing the slots or poker all weekend. His heart was with me. During our first years together, he would lie next to me, look into my eyes,

breathe my air, and tell me just how beautiful I was. Those were magical moments for me.

He saw me at my worst, smelled my morning breath, tried to understand me, and held on even after people around him suggested he shouldn't—all in the name of love. Now I am not going to pretend that it was all heavenly *all* the time, because Lord knows we had a whole host of other issues that are mentioned in other chapters. What I will say is that some of the actions he took made me believe he sincerely loved me. The guy who loves you shows you by how he acts, by what he is willing to do, and how he treats you and your loved ones. What he says, how he holds and kisses you, are important, as well. It seems almost impossible to get love, chemistry, and reciprocal feelings all at the same time. But, when you get it, you know it, and you feel it. But if there's doubt in your heart or mind about a person, honor that doubt. It may be the Universe trying to tell you something.

Know that there are men who prey on a woman's vulnerabilities. These men know we want and need them to love us to make us feel special and to accept our situations and our families. They know that we are built to be nurturers and we need protectors and providers. So they say the right things and often do the right things, at least initially. Their real intentions will unfold in due time. If you take enough time to get to know him, and ask the important questions about his life, his family, his ex-wife or girlfriend, his job, education, and background—not once but several times, in several different ways—the truth will emerge.

Last, when you're first getting to know him, if he offers you free trips or gifts or other things too good to be true, call his bluff to see what he actually does. With time, you will know if he is really looking for love or just a plain old-fashioned booty call.

Chapter 5

The Unbroken You

"Set fire to the broken pieces; start anew."

—Lauren DeStefano, *Sever*

Rhonda

Have you ever loved a man who abused you verbally or physically, yet you stayed with him? What about the man who wouldn't commit? Or that guy who was consistently inconsistent in what he showed you, yet you minimized it and held on? Ever loved someone who wouldn't love you back or would only give you bits and pieces of himself, yet no matter how much it tore at your spirit and made you cry, you allowed him to stay in your life and take up your time? Have you ever been cheated on by your spouse or significant other, not once, twice or three times but repeatedly—yet you stayed? This is what we do when we operate in unworthiness. This is what happens when our reservoir of self-love is at low levels, when we don't feel good in our own skin, don't believe we are capable of better and when we live in fear. And this is what happens when we don't trust our ability to live without *him* even when the relationship doesn't uplift our soul or our circumstances. This is the epitome of being *broken*.

The purpose in writing this brief chapter is to call attention to how the impact of what we believe about ourselves, is what either brings positive dating experiences into our lives or keeps us in unfulfilling, stagnant, non-productive situations with men who give the bare minimum, don't put their best forward and don't respect us. It is also to encourage you to strive toward being whole before you date that next guy or enter into a relationship.

It's a safe bet that you can go through your entire life *thinking like a man*, trying all the dating and relationship tricks known to man (and woman), and reading every self-help book in Barnes and Noble, but if you are operating on empty, living with the weighty memories and pain of the past, carrying baggage from what people have said to or about you and you can't look in the mirror with a smile, loving the woman looking back at you, odds are the relationship patterns you have will continue.

Iyanla Vanzandt entitled her latest book *Peace from Broken Pieces*; that title alone pulls you in. It details her broken life pieces, her negative belief systems, and how those feelings and thoughts caused her to lose *herself* in relationships, give away all of her power, and suffer immensely in every area of her life until she understood how those thoughts and actions impacted her choices, and it reveals how only after recognizing this that she found the courage and strength to re-group and find her way back to Spirit and wholeness. One of the most poignant quotes in her book was: "When two broken people, bring their broken pieces together, chances are they will never be a whole anything." She touched on something close to home and critically important for so many of us. When it comes to relationships, it matters much if we come into them *whole*, with our spirits soaring high and our self-esteem levels on full, or if we come in to them needy, empty, and not feeling worthy. If you are broken, you are in trouble before you ever connect with anyone, before you ever go on a first date with Mr. Wonderful. It's like setting out on a 3,000-mile road trip in your car and you have three flat tires, no gas, a headlight out, and engine problems.

The closer you are to feeling and being whole, the better you are going to be at navigating the dating game and eventually marriage. When people ask me what happened to my marriage and why it didn't work out, I openly tell them, "I was broken, I didn't have healthy self-esteem. I didn't know what being a wife meant. I didn't know what I wanted or needed in a husband. I had no examples of healthy love to reference at that time. And I had been violated so many times by people I should have been able to trust, that I didn't feel lovable." I came to my husband in pieces. I started my lifetime road trip with him without any of the necessary equipment or parts to make it on the journey for the long haul. We crashed and burned and I had to be repaired.

"Here's what is truly at the heart of wholeheartedness: Worthy now, not if, not when, we're worthy of love and belonging now. Right this minute. As is."

—Brené Brown, *The Gifts of Imperfection: Let Go of Who You Think You're Supposed to Be and Embrace Who You Are*

Many of us are lugging around our perceived unworthiness, we are carrying those hurtful words from the people who told us we were too fat, too skinny, too this too that, not good enough, not smart enough, not pretty enough, etc. We are carrying heartbreak, un-forgiveness, those images of being violated and the associated anger and resentment. And this is what prevents us from dating smart, seeing the obvious red flags, and it's also what causes us to ignore our intuition when we are getting to know people. Under these conditions, we see and hear what we need most, we cling to how good it sounds when he speaks and we get caught up in images (I have a boyfriend, or a husband), too often missing the truth of his intentions, treatment of you and character. We are so thirsty for our reservoirs to be filled that we buy into the mirage out in the hot desert sand, from the distance it looks like a refreshing body of water but up close, it's just an illusion. Our mind plays tricks on us when we are thirsty, needy. We go from one relationship to the next in search of that connection and someone to fill us up, make us happy and complete us. Each one leaving us more drained than the last.

Iyanla said: "Unworthiness always puts you in debt to anyone and everyone who shows you the slightest degree of love or attention or energy . . ." Let me give you some real life examples of this.

I know of a twenty-seven-year-old young lady, whom I will call Brenda (not her real name, she and I are too close to share her real name). She is a fitness buff, runs 5K's, eats healthier than anyone I know, and takes great care of her body. She is attractive, slim, and seems to be happy and balanced from the outside looking in. Two years ago, she met a man from the gym that she goes to; he was the tall, well-built and popular guy whom all the girls liked. He was single, she was single, they started dating, and for about three weeks it seemed like a match made in heaven. Then one day they had a disagreement about something, and out of nowhere he began to call her degrading names like "bitch," "hoe," etc., and it was during this time that he would periodically let her know she was "not quite pretty enough" and that she was lucky to be with him. The disagreements and outbursts would always settle and usually end with him apologizing for his comments and him telling her "she shouldn't make him that mad so that it wouldn't happen again."

They continued to date, a few more months went by, and his outbursts continued. She dismissed them as, "that's just what he does when he gets angry." She kept seeing him, and believed that the relationship was headed in a particular direction. One night, while visiting his house, she saw his cell phone on the counter while she was in the kitchen getting something to drink. The phone rang and she noticed a woman's name on the caller ID. She didn't answer the call, but when the phone stopped ringing, she picked it up and saw that he had lots of text messages from other women. Some of the strings of messages revealed that he had been seeing more than one other woman intimately.

This broke her heart, so she confronted the boyfriend who then went into a tirade. He yelled, screamed and demeaned her, calling her names and letting her know she had once again pissed him off. Finally, he yelled, "Get out of my house!" She left crying. Still, the relationship continued. She did everything she could to hold on to him, while telling me about all of the incidents. She stayed the course, not detoured at all by his mean words, angry outbursts or disrespect. A few months later, she found out that she was pregnant. She was delighted, he not so much. This wasn't part of his plan; after all he was only twenty-five and was living a very carefree life. Together, they decided to keep the baby and make things work. She gave up her house and they moved in together. To make a long, sad story short, the pregnancy didn't defuse his rage and anger. Bit by bit he continued the destruction of her self-esteem, telling her almost weekly that she was unattractive and kicking her out of the house whenever he felt like it. (While he had bought it, she paid all the bills.) Despite all the tears, tension and disrespect, she couldn't let him go.

Eventually their beautiful baby girl arrived. The madness got worse, and even an innocent child didn't stop his angry outbursts. Brenda was in love and wanted desperately to have a cohesive family. She told me, "I want my daughter to grow up with both parents."

For two years I watched this situation go from bad to worse. He had stolen the rosiness from her cheeks and the joy from her life. She rarely smiles anymore. She lost a great deal of weight after the baby was born, looking almost skeletal; she might be a size zero now. This is a woman who has a good career, great credit and options. I later learned she came from a family that shamed their children continually, didn't hug or show affection, and never said "I love you." She is operating in broken-ness. All the advice, recommendations and experience sharing in the world won't change this. She has to get tired of how it feels to be treated poorly; then and only then will it get better.

There is a woman whom I will call MaryAnn who has been married for thirty years. She and her husband have two children. They live in a high-end neighborhood, drive nice cars, eat at the best restaurants and wear the designer clothes and jewelry. MaryAnn's husband is a top 2 percent wage earner; he provides well for the family. He dotes on his children and is an intelligent, ambitious man who gets it done. However, MaryAnn's husband has cheated on her at least four or five times in thirty years, that she is aware of—and this number came from her mouth. In several of those situations, she has discovered it first hand, by finding him in action or at the other woman's house. She has also met several of the women and had the "conversation" threatening them to "leave her husband alone, or else." Yet, no matter how many times he cheats, she stays. After finding out, she cries, screams, and threatens to go, only to settle right back into the marriage. She is constantly checking his phone, emails and calling him when he is out of town on business. She calls his hotel room in the wee hours of the morning, to see if he will answer, and to keep control of the situation.

When I look at MaryAnn's situation I can't help but ask, how many times her trust must be violated and her heart broken for her to get the courage to leave? What is she holding on to? I don't know the inner most workings of their issues, I don't know when the cheating started or why, but I do know for sure that if your man cheats on you *that* many times, and you are not in an "open" relationship, something is terribly wrong with the relationship, or at minimum, something is missing. Neither party can be "happy" under these conditions. I am assuming here, but I think people who cling to this type of relationship cannot feel good, whole, or worthy.

"I believe that owning our worthiness is the act of acknowledging that we are sacred. Perhaps embracing vulnerability and overcoming numbing is ultimately about the care and feeding of our spirits"

—Brené Brown

When you are spiritually or emotionally broken you see things through a shattered prism. You only see bits and pieces of the picture. You are paralyzed by fear. You live in fear of losing, fear of not being enough, fear of someone leaving, fear of someone taking what you have, fear of speaking up when you need to say something. You are always on edge, and your judgment is off so you end up having people in your life who clearly aren't good for you: people who take more than they give, who aren't faithful or reliable, people who demean and disrespect you, who don't lift you up. Being "whole' changes that.

I speak from experience. In many of the relationships I have had over the years, marriage included, I never felt good enough or comfortable being me. I was afraid to set boundaries or standards. I was always afraid of being alone. I masked much of my anxiety and doubt in promiscuous behavior or by coming off as tough ("I don't need a man" tough) or I pretended that nothing and no one mattered—until it did matter and I felt I was losing someone important and that's when all hell would break loose.

Living afraid makes you crazy. You don't let your guard down, you don't love fully, you can't be vulnerable, your judgment is off and you are always in search of someone new to fill the void because after all it must be *them* and why bother looking inside? This is the antithesis of being whole.

Being whole is being able to tell someone, "What you did hurt me," or, "The fact that you were dishonest from the start, is something I cannot deal with," or, "Your inconsistency in calling or dating me is troubling and doesn't sit well with the direction I am going. I need consistency and since that isn't what you have to offer, I am willing to end this now and allow you to go about your business, so I can open up space for the person who brings that into my life." It's saying the truth without fear that he might not call again, or might not want to be in your life because you know the right one is on the way. You are able to date him, speak the truth, engage fully, be vulnerable, listen, and speak knowing that the right person for you will match your energy, and bring into your life, that which your soul needs to grow. It will have nothing to do with the game of thinking like your male counterpart and will have everything to do with embracing your complete self.

Connecting with the "unbroken you" is what is at the heart of the matter, and is the underlying theme throughout this book. There is no gimmick, no catchy words or phrases, just honest soulful discussion on how to date and relate from a position of wholeness.

Part Two

Getting What You Need from the Man You Are With

Chapter 6

Setting Standards with a Capital "S"

Shanae

This is the most important chapter that you will ever read in any relationship book. So get comfortable and pay very close attention.

One thing that I've learned over the years is that every successful business or idea that was manifested into something great, started off as a well thought out plan. When successful people want to accomplish something, they sit down and draw up a plan to accomplish their goals.

Did you know the gambling industry is the result of a well thought out plan? Have you ever gone to a casino and looked at the great pools, restaurants, nightclubs, spa facilities, the bright colors, the wide array of slot machines, and the card game tables? Do you know why the owners invest so much money into making casinos look grand? They do it to pull you in and entice you to play their game. They do it to get you caught up in the moment.

Casino owners look at the odds of each game that they plan to bring into the casino. They first weigh the cons and then determine the potential gain of every game they consider having on the casino floor. Next, the CEOs and gaming commissioners all get together and talk about how hard it would be to cheat at this game and what precautions need to be in place to limit the likelihood of an individual successfully cheating, or potentially ruining the integrity of the game itself. Needless to say, it can take several years after a game is introduced to a casino before it makes it to the casino floor. The reason for all of this is because the casino doesn't play to lose—they play to WIN! There is not a game in the casino that is being played that doesn't have a house advantage. Believe that. The house odds fluctuate depending on the type of game you are playing, but nonetheless they are all set up to draw a certain type of person—the rich, blue-collar workers, white-collar workers, the unemployed, the self-employed, annual visitors, or daily regulars. After the casino owners decide they want to have a certain game on the floor, they go through a careful process to determine the best way to win.

Ladies, that's what we want to do with this dating game. We have to reevaluate all the angles from which the game can be played . . . and PLAY TO WIN.

Identifying What You Want

Now let's seriously transfer this casino analogy into the game of LOVE, SEX, and MONEY (aka, "The Relationship Game"). In this game, you are the casino owner, the boss. The first step before adding this new game to your gaming lineup is to decide what kind of customer you are trying to attract. Remember, this is your game and you are the head person in charge (HPIC), so you can be as honest as you want. If you want a Brad Pitt or Denzel Washington look-alike, then say that. If you want a man with more muscles than Arnold Schwarzenegger in the eighties, then write it down. You are the ruler, and whatever rules you set should be followed. The point is, don't lower your standards for anyone during the building process. Again, this is your dream so don't shortchange yourself.

Let's have fun with this first step. We will call it the "my dream man" step. There should be at least three qualifying characteristics. Physical, spiritual, sexual, and financial would be good starting points. If you were going to put them on a chart, it might look something like this:

Name of Characteristics: (e.g., physical, sexual, financial)

My Perfect Man Would Be: (Ideal requirements go in the boxes)

Height:	Weight:	Skin Tone:	Other Qualities:	Type of Work:
6'0	190 lbs.	Dark Chocolate	Great Teeth	CEO of something

Each stage has its own chart, so list everything that is important to you. Each section is graded on a scale of 1 to 10 with 10 being the highest score. The person should have a minimum score of 80 percent before you even think about giving up the goodies. With a score of anything less, you are just wasting your time. All the items that he or she scored low on will eventually bother the hell out of you anyway. Take a moment to list your ideal person's requirements for each section. Fill in the chart with the people that you are already seeing or dating. It will clarify for you if this person is someone that you will be happy with later on in life.

Example: Physical Chart

Name	Height/ Score	Weight/ Score	Skin Tone/ Score	Teeth and/or Smile/ Score	Hygiene/ Score	Shoes/ Score	TOTAL SCORE
James	6'0"/10	180 lbs/ 8	Sexy brown/ 9	Perfect/ 10	9.5	10	56.5/60 = 94%
Stanley	5'8"/6	210 lbs/ 5	Bumpy/ 3	Straight /8	Musty /5	Dirty/ 7	34/60 = 56%

In comparing these two charts, Stanley is failing. We ain't going to make it. So, save the cell phone minutes and move on. But, if you really like someone as a person, such as Stanley, don't try to force a relationship, transfer him to the just friends category.

Name	Breath	Kissing	Affectionate	Penis Size	TOTAL SCORE
Stanley	9	8	7	Great, 10	34/40 = 85%
James	okay, 7	7	9	Small, 3	26/40 = 65%

Okay, I'm going to keep it real with you, sex weighs more than any other category (not really but you feel me). Again, if your potential man falls "short" and I'm not talking about height, this may be a nonnegotiable. He can be a lot of things, but being built like a six-year-old boy is not one; we ain't going to make it. I don't care how much money he has or how cute he is, the best we can ever be is friends.

After you list all of your wants and needs, you should split them into two columns and list the negotiable on one side and the nonnegotiable on the other side. Now have fun and fill in the names of guys that are on your list and see how closely they really match up to your requirements. You may be surprised how they look on paper.

Example: Moral/Spiritual

Name	Fears God	Goes to Church	Parents Are Together	Is He Married?	Honest
Chris	7	5	10	Yes, 1	2

This section is really all about your personal preference. However, it is definitely important that you ask the right questions about a person's history. For instance, if the man that you are seeing was exposed to violence as a kid; he is more likely to show abusive tendencies in your relationship. This section is really going to take a little more effort.

Identifying what you want in a man is pertinent to your success in finding a healthy relationship. When I was fifteen years old, I made a chart very similar to the one that follows. Of course at fifteen, my wish list lacked some of the more important qualities. My requirements at the time were:

Tall	
Brown Skin	
Athletically Built	
Nice Teeth	
Has A Car	
Plays Sports	
Good Kisser	
Good Dresser	
Attractive	

Lo and behold the man of my dreams had all the qualities on my list. He was tall, handsome, an athlete, had great teeth, a beautiful smile, and he had a car. Wow! But, he was also crazy! So make sure when you're putting your list together to add things like at peace, happy with himself, not needy or insecure, educated, and other important characteristics. You get the point. You want the Universe to put together the perfect man, leave no stone unturned. Write all of your wants down on paper and let the Universe do the rest.

Once you have been sent the man of your dreams, "The game" begins. Remember our earlier talk about how gambling CEOs and gaming commissioners get together to devise a plan that will ensure the best house advantage? Well, that's the next step—creating a game plan to your advantage.

The Dating Game

Let's assume he likes you and you like him. What do you do from here? You start dating. The first few dates are crucial to the direction of the relationship. It is in the beginning of the relationship that you must establish (1) your expectations, (2) what you are willing to sacrifice, and (3) what kind of time and attention you demand. Make sure your first date is somewhere that you will enjoy. If he thinks Red Lobster is the spot and you're thinking hell no, say that, in a polite way. Let him know when you don't like something and more important that he shouldn't expect to sleep with you on the first date.

I remember one time a platonic friend of mine that I had known for a while asked me to fly to Jamaica with him for the weekend. I needed to think about his question for a minute and told him that I would call him back. When I called him back, I asked him if we were going to have separate rooms. He paused for a moment and said, "Well, I didn't really think about that, but honestly, I can't see going to Jamaica with you and you sleeping in another room." I made it clear I didn't want to lose our friendship by becoming intimate. Because I expressed that we would have to have separate rooms, and he was honest about his intentions, we both agreed that Jamaica was probably not a good spot for platonic friends to go hang out. The more up front and honest you and your friends or potential partners are with each other, the faster the relationship will progress in the right direction.

Recently we interviewed a couple that had been married for eleven years. I asked the husband how he knew she was the one. The wife started laughing and said, "Tell her how you went from six girlfriends to one." He told us that his wife's standards were so high, that slowly, the other girls began to fall off because he couldn't afford her and everyone else. She ended up being the last woman standing and won the prize. Setting your standards and sticking to them will help you reach your relationship goals. It is also important to have an idea of how long you want to wait before you have sex when your dream man comes along and try to stick to it. Steve Harvey says wait ninety days. I can't say that there is a magic number, but make him wait. I know people who had sex the first night they met and decided to get married shortly thereafter. On the other hand, I also have a friend who had sex with another friend of mine on the first date, and the next night I watched him not even acknowledge her presence while we were at the restaurant. She sent him a text while we were all eating dinner, and he looked at his phone and put it away. He wouldn't even give her eye contact. It was the saddest, most disrespectful thing that I had ever seen. In short, refrain from having sex too early, and never go on a first date where there's a bed.

The Questions You Should Ask

You must ask questions, and lots of them. Steve Harvey's book lists five questions that all women should ask a man: (1) What are your long-term goals? (2) What are your short-term goals? (3) What are your views on relationships? (4) What do you think about me? (5) How do you feel about me? Mr. Harvey also advises, "There's no need to delay asking these questions—ask them right away, as soon as you think you might be remotely attracted to a man you've met" (p. 133).

With all due respect to Mr. Harvey, the first three questions are good, but the last two questions may not be realistic. Most women know how hard it is to get a man to be honest with them on the first date about something as simple as his marital status. So what are the odds of a man giving us an honest assessment (other than traditional complimentary things) of how he feels or thinks about us early on (or later on for that matter)? To test this out, we asked several men,while on a staged date, "What do you think about me?" and "What do you feel about me?" Here's what we found:

Shanae: "What do you think about me?"

Guy 1: "I think you are beautiful and you have a great body, and nice teeth."

Shanae: *[So, you really want to know if I'm good in bed?]* "How do you feel about me?"

Guy 1: [With a confused look on his face] "What do you mean?"

Shanae: "How do you feel about me?"

Guy 1: "Well, that's why we're here, so I can get to know you better. I really don't know enough about you to answer that."

I also asked a few of my male friends how they would respond if a girl asked them those questions. They all said they would tell her what they thought she wanted to hear. To further illustrate this point:

My friend Curtis and I were driving to the mall one day when he received a call from a girl "he liked." And I heard him lying to her about his relationship status and several other personal questions that she asked. When he got off the phone, I asked him, "Why did you lie to her?" He said that he never tells girls the truth, because if he did, they wouldn't let him *hit it*. "Girls need to think that they are the only one." He said, "I tell *you* the truth because I know that we're never going to have sex. But the other girls get exactly what they want to hear."

Our conclusion: Questions only work IF MEN ARE HONEST.

However, I do agree that we have to ask more questions, and that we should only ask the questions that are going to propel our relationships in a healthy direction.

All of the men we interviewed also said it's best to keep questions about sex and money to a minimum, at least initially. Keep in mind that the same things that make you laugh can make you cry. Similarly, the same questions you ask a man, he may also ask you. So before you speak, ask yourself, "Do I want him to ask me these same questions?" Here are some questions we think are absolutely imperative!

Questions you *should* ask early in the relationship:

1) Are you married? (He may lie, but at least you asked.)
2) Are you still friends with your baby's mama (e.g, your ex-wife, girlfriend, friend)?
3) What is your ideal woman? Describe her.
4) Do you want kids?
5) Do you have children?
6) How often do you see your children (if you have any)?
7) Are you close to your mom?
8) How often do you call/see your mom?
9) How long was your longest relationship?
10) How do you feel about love, sex, and monogamy?
11) If you were a box of cereal, which one would you be and why?
12) How do you feel about Internet dating?

If you ask these questions with a genuine, gentle tone—meaning not judgmental, and not attacking or grilling him, you will have greater success in getting honest, heartfelt answers. Hopefully, he will tell you everything you need to know. Let's discuss each question.

1) Are you married?

My girlfriend and I were having lunch at a small café in Studio City. We were engaging in our normal girl talk, when she said, "Shanae let me tell you about this married guy I dated." The first thing that I asked was, "Did you know he was married?" She said, "No!" and began to explain how they met and how she found out he was married. Before she could finish her story, I asked her, "Did you ask him if he was married when you met him?" She said, "No, I didn't know I had to ask if he was married. I assumed that if he was dating me, spending nights with me, traveling and going to business events with me, that he was single." She added, "I'm forty-nine years old. In my generation, married men don't date." I quickly responded by saying this is a new day. Today, you must ask!

2) Are you still friends with your baby's mama (e.g., your ex-wife, girlfriend, friend)?

Shanae

Remember, the child's mother can hold a very special place in his heart, especially if he ever loved her. I like to ask this question because if he is still heartbroken over his ex, he is probably not ready to give himself to you, and this relationship could end up being more work than it's worth. I am not in the business of helping men get over their ex or dating men who are still intimate with their ex. When you ask this question, listen very closely to the answer and the tone in his voice. When you ask, "Are you still friends with your baby's mama?" and he says something like, "Hell no, I can't stand her crazy ass," then it is probably safe to assume that he is open to a new, healthy relationship. You should also ask, "What is it that makes her so crazy?" What you are looking for is if he did anything that might have made her "crazy." Think Elin Woods—Tiger Woods' wife.

If he answers the initial question with, "I didn't want to break up with her, she left me." He's not over her and you are probably just a rebound. If she never comes back to him, great, but if she changes her mind at any point and wants him back, you can kiss him goodbye. If he says, "We are cool, we just grew apart. I still have love for her . . . she's the mother of my kids. We're just two different people now, and I am looking for something else" then he is probably a keeper. You can move on to your next question.

Rhonda

Asking if he's still friends with his baby's mama is a very important question when trying to get to know someone. My ex-husband and I were both guilty of hurting people through our twenty-year course of breaking up and then making up. Other people really didn't have a chance until we were able to put our past behind us and move on with our individual lives. Even after divorce, we were still connected through our children, the homes we owned, and our business. Thus, we were forced to stay in close contact even when we didn't really want to be around one another. I know other women with similar stories. Unfortunately, the ex-woman usually still has some sort of advantage, like it or not. Ladies, these situations are dangerous for your heart. It is critically important that you listen closely, as Shanae suggested. Pay attention to his answers as well as his body language. Also pay attention to how he talks to her on the phone and how he treats you in her presence.

3) What is your ideal woman? Describe her.

Shanae

Ask him to describe his ideal or dream woman. If he describes someone that isn't you, let him go. This means he would be settling and your relationship will not last. When he finds that ideal person, he will move on to her.

Do you remember the guy Mark that I talked about in previous chapters? Well, I was so in love with Mark. He could sing, he was attractive, and he was attentive. Mark was super sexy and had everything I wanted in a man. I assumed I was his type (he asked me for my number) until I asked him to describe his ideal woman: "The first girl I ever had sex with was white. Since then, white women have been my preference." At that very moment I realized that I was a woman that he liked and cared for, but he didn't see me the same way that I saw him. His preference was someone that I was not, and could never be, if I had only asked sooner. Everything that I am telling you, I learned the hard way. If only one person reads this and learns from it, then this book has done its job.

Rhonda

A very good friend of mine shared a story with me that adds creditability to the importance of this question. In looking at the type of women her ex-husband dated when they broke up (typically white or Hispanic), and in reading some of the online profiles he posted on Internet dating sites, she said she was shocked to discover he was attracted to women of other races, shapes, and ages none of which resembled her. She said to me, "I was shocked to learn that his age preference was anywhere from thirty to forty-two, his race preference ranged from no preference to Latin and white, and he solicited women with specific physical attributes like "athletic." None of those descriptors described my friend. So this lovely African American, medium-built woman who was in her mid-forties was left to wonder if her ex-husband always had those desires, or did he simply develop them after they broke up? It could be that he always loved her like she was at that time, then changed. Who really knows? Either way, you see the importance of asking questions in the beginning, particularly this one.

4, 5, 6) Do you want kids? Do you have children? How often do you see them?

Shanae

Whether you have children or not, these questions tell you a lot about the man that you are dating. From these short questions, you will be able to determine if he is responsible, if he is proud of his family (whether the kids where planned or not), and if he is selfish and thinks the world rotates around him. If he says he doesn't have any kids, then go to the next question.

If he is over 37 and doesn't have any kids, that is a red flag for me. Why? Because it tells me one of four things: (1) He can't have children, (2) he has supported an ex-wife or ex-girlfriend in having an abortion, (3) he is selfish and doesn't want anything or anyone that is going to take money from him, or (4) he's on the down low (we won't go there). If you ask him if he has kids and he says yes, and then tells you their ages and how many, this is a very good sign. That means he is proud of his family and no matter what the situation is with the mother of his children, he is making it known that they are a part of him.

Rhonda

It is key to know what kind of father he is to his own kids. Does he spend quality time with them? Does he offer them sound advice? Does he care about their education? Is he concerned about their accomplishments and goals? Does he feel it's important to be involved in helping to shape their overall character and spirituality? While we expect women who have children to want their men to have kids, too, others prefer for him not to have children of his own. There are women with children, who actually want men who don't have kids, to avoid "baby mama drama." These women were also concerned that if the man had kids, his responsibilities to and for his children may impact the quality and quantity of time with her. Whether you are for or against a man with kids, knowing whether he has kids is the first step toward getting past this dating hurdle. Because I am a mother who has already raised three children and still has a teenage son to rear, it's important for me to date a man who understands parenting. Perhaps he would be able to offer sound advice and serve as a role model and father figure to my son.

7, 8) Are you close to your mom? How often do you call/see your mom?

Shanae

It seems like such a simple question, with such a simple answer, but it says so much. Think about it. If he doesn't respect or care enough about the woman who gave birth to him, he probably isn't going to care or respect you very much. On the other hand, if he doesn't know his mom, or didn't grow up with a woman in the house, there is going to be a gap in his relationship with you. This is something that you want to know up front. The more questions you ask, the fewer surprises you will have to deal with later.

Rhonda

If a man can't love his mama, can't forgive his mama, doesn't talk to or see his mama, run! Even if she wasn't the best mom and even if she wasn't there as often as he thinks she should have been, that man must be able to talk about those things and tell you the story. You have to be able to see that he has mended those wounds or is actively working through how he feels about his mom and that he can work through the remnants of his past, perhaps with you. The dynamics of the mother-son relationship is key to the success of your relationship.

9) How long was your longest relationship?

Shanae

This section only applies to people over twenty-five. This question helps to identify a man's level of commitment. If he says, "I was with my last girl for ten years," and he didn't marry her, it's because she wasn't the one but he found it easier to settle for someone that he didn't want rather than to leave her alone so that she can find someone who did want to marry her and continue his journey solo. In short, this man may be selfish. If he says, "I was married to my ex-wife for *x* number of years," ask how long it took before he married her. If he provides an answer that is less than six months that tells you he is impatient (or fell madly in love). If he says two to three years, he's practical. Two to three years is the average amount of time for a couple to date before getting married. If he says four to seven years, that means he's very cautious and doesn't trust easily (or wasn't ready to give up the players card just yet). Trying to make him bond with you before he is ready, is going to be time consuming, energy draining, and the relationship is probably going to fall apart anyway. If he says, "I have never been in a real relationship," find out why you may be the one to change that.

Rhonda

Great response Shanae!! That pretty much sums it up on this one.

10) How do you feel about sex, love, and monogamy?

Rhonda

This is probably the most important question to ask a man. We can all assume how a man feels about sex. But asking him what he feels about sex provides him the opportunity to talk sex while looking you in your eyes, fully dressed. Asking such questions will help you to determine if he places any value on sex, if he practices safe sex, and if he is selective in his choice of women. If he says "sex is just sex," or "I just get it in where I can," then you already know what to do. If he is in love with you or has some sort of emotional connection to you, he may see sex in a different light. Once sexual intercourse takes place, the relationship will either deepen or fall apart. Every woman reading this knows what I am talking about, but how many of us have sat in front of the man we are dating and asked him this question? I didn't ask this question the first twenty years of my life, but today I most certainly do.

When it comes to love, ask him when was the last time he was "in love" and how did he know? Ask him what love means to him and what does it feel like when he's in love. Ask him what's different about being in love and just dating a girl he likes. Listen to what he says, and watch his body language. Look into his eyes and search for honesty and truth. By asking this question, you are hoping to find out if he has been in love or not, what made him fall in love (other than the obvious chemistry and things in common), and what was it about the previous woman he loved so much. This also allows you to identify whether he's capable of having strong feelings for a woman or not.

Monogamy. For those of you (us) who want or expect a monogamous relationship, this is an important question to ask. This is also the time for you to discuss your expectations with him. Let him know if you expect to have a monogamous relationship or if an "open" relationship is acceptable.

11) If you were a box of cereal, which one would you be and why?

Shanae

This is a fun question to ask because it tells you how men perceive themselves. I will never forget when I was first asked that question. I was eighteen years old and interviewing for a job, my future boss asked me this question. I said, "Captain Crunch, I am sweet like the sugar coating, a leader like a captain, and crunchy," and we both fell out laughing. I couldn't think of anything else. On my way home, I was so disappointed that I couldn't think of a better cereal. Plus, Captain Crunch scrapes the roof of your mouth. However, I did get the job. During our first training session, he explained why he had asked that question, and said the best answer he ever received was Grape Nuts. The person who gave the Grape Nuts answer said he chose that cereal because it's strong and consistent, even in milk. I learned that the type of cereal is not important. It's why a person picks a certain cereal that's important. If the man you are thinking about dating says, Fruity Pebbles, regard his answer as a HUGE RED FLAG and run for the hills.

12) How do you feel about Internet dating?

Rhonda

Let's face it, Internet dating is here to stay; match.com, blackpeoplemeet.com, plentyoffish.com, and a host of other dating sites provide easy avenues for people to find friends, love, and sex. If you find your mate on one of these sites, be sure to follow up when you start dating to make sure he or she has abandoned the old user ID and is only dating you. Also, if you are married, living with someone, or otherwise in a committed relationship, it behooves you to periodically check the computer to see what could be happening right there in front of your eyes. To further illustrate this point, I was recently in the hair salon, and began a conversation with a lady in her mid-forties who said she had recently gotten married (within the last two years). She said this was her first marriage and the guy was a few years younger than her.

We were all excited for her. Salivating at the details. Then she told us her newlywed saga. She said that her new husband had established a Facebook account and was representing himself as a single man. There were no pictures of her or his family posted on his page and his social status was, "single, interested in women." She also learned that he was on a popular dating site. When she confronted her husband, he said he was just trying to meet new friends. While he was at work and home alone, he said he sometimes got a "little bored and needed to be entertained." WTF? He also decided he no longer needed to wear his wedding ring and began going out solo and staying out late. She eventually found the text messages and e-mails that confirmed her worst fears. She was hurt and angry. She said she waited her whole life to get married and never imagined that while she was away at work, her husband was searching cyberspace for women.

There are women on these sites who are legitimately looking for a man, others who post partially naked photographs of themselves are obviously looking for something else. To the men who see these photos, they convey quick access to conversation and ass. This is a part of dating in the Information Age. Keep your husbands close and the computers closer.

Chapter 7

Why Did I Get Married?

Shanae

Every engaged, married, and divorced woman must honestly ask herself, “Why do I want to marry this person?” or “Why did I get married?”

Before I answered this question, I needed to talk to some guys and hear their answers. I didn’t understand why so many married men I knew cheated, so I decided to interview them and hear their story. One day, a friend of mine and I were talking, and I asked him why he got married. He said, “She was the best pick for the long haul. She’s a great mother, she’s sexy, she doesn’t curse, eat meat, drink alcohol, or go clubbing. She’s a perfect wife.” I said, “But you cheat, drink, and smoke. How does that work?” “I know,” he said. “She doesn’t enjoy the same things that I do, so I find women who I am more compatible with to do the things she doesn’t do.” WTF?

I have another married male friend who swears he is single. I asked him how he managed to have several serious relationships, over the past ten years, while still married. He said, “Well, I just realized I was unhappy.”

So I asked him, "Why did you marry your wife?" He said he married her because they had the same financial vision, and she was very smart. WTF? The last time I checked, that was not a reason to get married.

Another male friend of mine, named Ray, dated one of my girlfriends. Ray was also married. When I asked Ray why he cheated on his wife, he said, "Because my wife, on her best day, is a seven (on a scale of one to ten). On a regular day, she's a five or six, and I simply enjoy being with beautiful women." He also said, "I don't have any plans to leave her. She's a great wife, but I don't have any plans to be faithful either." That's some cold stuff right there. Go ahead and say it—WTF?

I can honestly say that I got married for love, maybe at the wrong time, but unequivocally for love. My husband-to-be and I met when I was fourteen. I knew we were going to get married someday. He was everything I wished for in my dreams: extremely gorgeous, nice teeth and a great smile, beautiful, milk chocolate skin, tall, and athletic. We started dating, and I loved everything about him—his broken fingers, his scars, his breath (good or bad). I loved it all. We dated for about a year and then broke up my sophomore year of high school. Cory was a senior.

Shortly after our breakup, he got into a fight at school and had to finish his last year at a different high school. We were apart for a year or so, and during that short period of time Cory got another girl pregnant. It hurt like hell. All of my thoughts were now about Cory, the other girl, and now a baby. When I asked about the baby, Cory lied and said it wasn't his baby. The following year we started dating again. I was a junior in high school, and Cory was a freshman in college.

About six months into our relationship, he called me and said the baby was his. The blood test was positive. Although my first instinct was to break up with him, he somehow convinced me to stay. This would be the beginning of many years of lies and tears.

One Friday afternoon, in 1997, I drove to Fresno to visit Cory at college. He and his roommate Chuck had to go somewhere, and I stayed behind at their house. I was watching television in the living room when the phone rang in Chuck's room. After so many rings, the answering machine picked up and the voice on the other end said, "Hey, Cory, this is Ruth. Give me a call, but before the female caller could hang up the phone, I rushed into Chuck's room, and picked up the phone, "Hi, this is Shanae. How do you know Cory?" I asked circumspectly. I remembered Cory mentioning her name to me before, but wasn't quite sure about the nature of their relationship. Ruth immediately knew who I was, and told me all the things that she knew about me. She also told me that she and Cory had been intimate. I asked her specifically if they had sex, she didn't answer.

Since the answering machine was never turned off, the entire conversation was recorded. As soon as he and Chuck came home, I furiously walked him into Chuck's room and pressed play. He heard the entire conversation, and began explaining his side of the story. I asked all the normal questions any girlfriend would ask. "Who is she?" and "Why is she calling you?" I asked. "Did you have sex with her?" Angry and frustrated, Cory grabbed my neck and began to choke me. Chuck sat on the sofa and played video games. He eventually said, "Man, don't choke her." Then Cory released me.

Crying, I ran into his room and slammed the door behind me. Why did he choke me? What did I do to deserve that? About an hour later and without an apology, Cory came into the room and said I shouldn't have been in Chuck's room in the first place. At seventeen, I didn't see the red flag. I was so caught up in our love (or lust) that I lost track of the difference between right and wrong. For the young and old who may be reading this and can relate, a man putting his hands on you is wrong (always) and it doesn't get better with time.

In September of 1998 I found out I was pregnant. Cory and I had been living together for nearly a year. I was a sophomore in college, and he was a senior. Less than a year later, Cory was drafted into the NFL by the Cincinnati Bengals. Our daughter, Nya, was born on June 7,1999. Recently drafted into the NFL and fearful of having to pay too much child support to his first child's mother, Cory decided to start a relationship with her again. Of course he failed to seek my knowledge or approval.

In early December 2000, I received child support papers from the California Department of Social Services (keep in mind our wedding was scheduled for December 31, 2000). The mother of Cory's first child was requesting more money. I asked him if he had been paying her according to their agreement. He said, "Yes!" and that he would handle it and not to worry. I thought to myself, if she was receiving money every month, why was she filing for child support? It didn't make sense so I called her to ask. She said she filed because the child support payments were not being sent on time every month and the amount sent some months was less than others. I then asked her if I took the responsibility to send the payments every month, would that make her feel more comfortable. She said, "What do you mean? Do you live there?" I told her yes, and asked what she meant. She said Cory told her I didn't live with him.

I turned on the recorder of my phone to record the remainder of our conversation. She said he flew her to Cincinnati twice. One of those times was for Mother's Day. After she and I got off of the phone, I promptly placed our daughter in her car seat and drove to the training facility where Cory was at practice with the team. When I arrived, I saw one of Cory's teammates and asked him to go get him. Cory came out, and I played the tape of my conversation. He told me she was crazy and that it never happened. I didn't believe him. He had to get back to work so I left. He came home early from practice to check on me. I was still furious and crying. "That's what you get for listening to her crazy ass. You let her do this to you," he said. He even shed a tear and asked how I could let these lies come into our home! Curious, I called her back. This time she provided irrefutable details like dates, times, where he was, where they stayed, the car he drove, and most importantly, her flight information.

He came downstairs, and heard me speaking on the house phone, while I was still talking to her, and hung up the phone. I cried and cried and cried. Talk about being devastated. I loved Cory, but this day changed my life, my relationship with him, and the way that I saw him, forever. When I asked him, "Why?" he said, "It was cheaper than paying her court awarded child support." In the end, the courts only awarded her an additional $1,000 per month. It was pennies comparatively speaking.

Why did I get married anyway? My wedding date was now only three weeks away. We had already spent thousands of dollars for the wedding, and I didn't want to lose the money. We also had a daughter, and I didn't want to be a single parent. I figured I would be taken care of financially, and I was already comfortable with Cory. I wish I would have had NBA player, Richard Jefferson, to counsel me nine years ago. I went down the altar and said "I do" when I didn't.

After the reception, we came back to our apartment in Fresno. He seemed so happy, and I felt so sad, hurt, and angry. I didn't feel anything like I thought I would feel on my wedding day. The "fairy tale" had begun and ended all at the same time. Long story short I filed for divorce in 2007. Although I regret getting married before getting help, I learned some difficult lessons, and Cory and I remain friends and focused parents to our children.

What doesn't kill you, only makes you stronger.

Rhonda

There was a time in my life early on when being married and having a diamond ring felt right and in my mind it proved my man's love and commitment to me. It meant everything. In looking at the state of relationships today, my own included, I now can't help but wonder what exactly a "ring" proves, prevents, or establishes? I note that Mr. Harvey so kindly dedicated a chapter in his prior book that tells us "how to get the ring." I admire that chapter and its intent. However, before I go into answering why I got married, I have to ask something that is bugging the hell out of me regarding the "ring." What does it mean to get a ring? What did it prove for Halle Berry, Sandra Bullock, and so many others? Does a ring guarantee a lifelong monogamous relationship? No. Does a ring ensure respect, protection from abuse, emotional and financial support, and unconditional love? No. Does it shelter one from heartbreak? No. Today, more often than not, a ring is merely a symbol of marriage devoid of meaning. Sure it can mean that in the event of his death, as his wife, you get the insurance benefits and social security payments but then that isn't why we marry is it? There was a time when "the ring" meant you were marrying your soulmate—the man who would love, honor, cherish, and provide for you, and be faithful until death. Today, however, it seems to represent a bond between two people that only lasts until one pisses the other off one too many times, the woman becomes unattractive to the man, money gets tight, or until another woman in a short skirt with a big ass and some double D's comes along. When that happens, he seems to forget about the ring, the commitment, the kids, and everything else the unbroken circle of gold, platinum, or silver was supposed to signify.

Unfortunately, so many wives before, during, and after this book will learn or will have learned that *the ring* simply means she possesses what is hopefully a very nice piece of jewelry on her finger. So make sure it's a good cut, with great clarity and size, in the event he strays, falls out of love, or otherwise violates his vows. Let there be enough equity in that bad boy to sell it or pawn it so you can take yourself on a nice post-relationship vacation and fund your divorce party.

I'm not saying meaningful and lasting proposals and marriages don't exist—I still believe there are some. What I am saying, however, is the ring, in and of itself, signifies nothing. As we have said throughout this book, you need more than a ring, you need the man's heart. It is also important to know his relationship with God, with himself, and with his mama.

My point is, don't fall for the illusion that getting that diamond or band means you have won the lottery and that life is set. Look at the women who have come before you, whose stories are all around you, and learn from their experiences. Enjoy your precious moments but remain aware and not caught up in the clouds.

Now back to the question, "Why did I get married?" I got married because I was in *love* with a capital "L" and I was broken with a capital "B." Plus, I had two young, beautiful daughters who needed a stable father figure. I had never felt chemistry like I did with my (now ex) husband. It was euphoric, amazing, sexy, and it made me forget about everything that was wrong in my life. I was looking to my husband to save me from my life, from my disconnectedness, and to make me feel loved (not the best reasons).

My ex was handsome, physically fit, and seemed kind. He was somewhat shy and quiet, but sexy. He was a gentleman. He opened doors for me and treated me like a lady. He seemed genuine. He was in the U.S. Air Force and was stable.

I was a mother of two at the time, and although he had contributed to the birth of a son, while overseas in the military, he lacked the experience of being a dad. He seemed okay with the idea of a "ready made family" for a while, but the days, months, and years ahead would prove otherwise.

We both came from troubled backgrounds. He came from a family of seven sisters, a wonderful, Christian mom, and a hardworking but jealous dad who had physically abused his mother on more than one occasion. I came from a family of five siblings, three brothers and two sisters, and a dysfunctional background too lengthy and disturbing to talk about. I saw my father twice while growing up, and my mom was often emotionally unstable. She married three times, was involved in a few tumultuous relationships, and struggled to find love most of her life. This left an indelible impression on me, which ultimately affected my relationships with men. Though I don't blame her or hold her accountable, it was the starting point, the place where I developed standards for myself and for those I chose to love.

I married and divorced the same guy twice, and we dated off and on after each divorce. I was too afraid to let him go and be alone. Our marriage contained infidelity, out-of-control rage, and periodic emotional abuse. Unfortunately, when you are broken in spirit; lack a solid foundation of family values and principles; missing a clear example of what a stable marriage should look and feel like; and are unsure how to juggle being a wife, a mother, and a career-oriented woman, you are sure to run into trouble. This is true especially when your husband is just as troubled as you are. I want you to ask yourself a few questions. What is your story? Why did you get married? When you think of your husband or the guy you are dating, how would you answer the following question, "If I were financially stable, emotionally and spiritually sound, in great physical shape, and had a great support system, would I still be with this guy?" If you can honestly say yes, then you are probably in the right situation. If, however, your answer is "Hell to-the-no!!" or a milder version of that, then perhaps you married for the wrong reasons. It's imperative that you examine where you are, how you got there, and what you're going to do about it.

The key is to find out why you and your husband married or why you and your significant other are thinking about marriage. If it was or is for superficial reasons like, fear, insecurity, or to be with someone until something better comes along, you may want to re-evaluate your situation. I learned this the hard way.

Chapter 8
Understanding Your Baggage

The past lives in you as memories, but memories in themselves are not a problem. In fact, it is through memory that we learn from the past and from past mistakes. It is only when memories, that is to say, thoughts about the past, take you over completely that they turn into a burden, turn problematic, and become part of your sense of self. Your personality, which is conditioned by the past, then becomes your prison. Your memories are invested with a sense of self, and your story becomes who you perceive yourself to be. (Tolle, 2008, p. 140)

The perception we have of ourselves is what has the potential to destroy our ability to enter into relationships worthy of our time and commitment. When you first read the title of this chapter, you probably thought, "Baggage?" You might have even thought, "Okay, I have a little debt, a few too many kids, and I could stand to go to the gym to shrink this pouch. Well, that's surface level baggage. We are going to take it a little deeper and talk about the baggage we carry *within* us.

Shanae

At the end of my marriage, I knew that I had healing to do. No matter what people say, it takes two people to have a great relationship, and one person to destroy it. When people that we love do things that hurt us over and over again, it is human nature to build up some form of a defense system. Some people will become very angry with the world, some will go through life always playing the victim role. I chose to heal and live a great life, but I knew that I needed to acknowledge that I was wounded and only time and God would allow me to heal properly.

Shortly after Cory and I separated, I recognized that I carried a lot of baggage and pain as residue from our marriage. When I looked in the mirror, all I saw was "little me" who had been picked on, mistreated, and who had an extraordinary hill to climb if I ever wanted to be in a healthy trusting relationship again. There are so many stories that come to mind that I could share with you as an example of things that men do that hurt us and leave permanent scars, but one particular incident, that happened to me really sticks out.

It was a Wednesday night in March, my husband was in Florida, training for his seventh season in the NFL. The kids and I were still in Georgia continuing our daily routine of school, work, and sports. This particular night I had tucked the kids in bed early so I decided to surf the Web for a few minutes before I went to bed. The computer was already logged into Cory's AOL account so I decided to use it as my browser. As I was surfing the net, I noticed an unfamiliar name in the Buddies Box. I clicked on the name and started an IM (instant messaging) chat. I typed "hi," and waited for a response. "Your wife must be upstairs, asleep. You already told me good night. What are you still doing up?" was the response I received back. I continued to talk to her as if I were Cory. She proceeded to tell me (Cory) she loved me, she would take care of me, and that she didn't understand why I kept trying to make it work with my wife. For twenty-five minutes she told me about "our" relationship (my marriage). Then she asked me (Cory), how I felt about her. I told her I had to go. She was pissed. She said I made her expose herself and then didn't answer the question. So, of course, she's calling him at the same time I'm calling him. She kept instant messaging me (Cory), telling me to answer the phone.

When he became aware of the situation, Cory caught the next flight home. After I heard his lame-ass story, I sat on the bedroom floor with my laptop and pulled up his phone bill online with him in the room, and pointed out all of their phone calls. Some of which were as long as five hours in one day. Most of them were forty-five minutes, a couple of times a day. Quick tempered, Cory jumped up out of his chair, smashed the laptop with his foot, and threw me around the house for an hour. He said I should have just stopped while I was ahead.

When he got tired, he said he was going back to Florida and left. I called the police and they immediately issued a warrant for his arrest. He turned himself in, and guess who bailed him out? You guessed it; I did. I bailed out the man who had just assaulted me. After he was released, Cory stayed at a friend's house for a few days and then came home. About a week later, we got into another big argument. This time, I told him to pack his shit and leave. He said he wasn't going anywhere. Needing to prove to him that I had the upper hand, I went down to the courthouse, filed a restraining order, and came back to the house with seven police officers. They gave him ten minutes to get as much as he could and leave the house. They also made him leave his opener to the entry gate, his garage door opener, and all the keys to the house. Looking back, I could have handled things differently. I could have left. I should have sought help. I am not saying he was right, I am just saying that I added fuel to the fire every chance I got. I wanted Cory to understand that I was going to pay him back for every time he hurt me, every time he lied to me, and every time he made me cry. My ego was in full gear, and I sought revenge. The last two years of our marriage were not sexy. I suffered and my children suffered unnecessarily.

Then one day I realized I was tired of fighting. I realized my ego was not as big as his desire to win, even if it meant losing in the end.

Eckhart Tolle says it so eloquently in *A New Earth*:

Very unconscious people experience their own ego through its reflection in others. When you realize that what you react to in others is also in you (and sometimes only in you), you begin to become aware of your own ego. At that stage, you may also realize that you were doing to others what you thought others were doing to you. You cease seeing yourself as the victim . . . You are not the ego, so when you become aware of the ego in you, it does not mean you know who you are—it means you know who you are not. But it is through knowing who you are not that the greatest obstacle to truly knowing yourself is removed (p. 189).

It is our job as women to find out what internal baggage we carry. This is important because it is virtually impossible to have a healthy relationship when we are unconsciously seeking drama and chaos. My life has gone from fighting, crying, and arguing every day to peace, quiet, and days full of joy and laughter. I had to re-evaluate myself to find my true sense of tranquility. Obviously, I had to undergo a lot of spiritual uplifting to get to the mental space I'm in now, but there is no other place I would rather be. My entire soul and spirit are now at peace. Sometimes just saying, "I'm tired and I deserve better," is half the battle. Getting on the right path and finding your way is the other half.

Rhonda

The journey toward identifying our own baggage is sometimes very challenging and scary. Looking in the mirror and evaluating our flaws is something most of us don't want to do. I certainly didn't want to see mine. It was far easier to look outside myself and point the finger than to go within. We often seek to blame other people, including men, for the breakdowns, the BS, and the state of our lives, particularly if where we are is not where we want to be. This doesn't mean the blame isn't justified toward the other party, it simply means, the blame mirror should be fully extended to show the full view of both parties.

I can remember my husband and the guys I dated making comments like, "You don't respect me when we are out in clubs. You don't know how to act," or "You feed off the attention of other men." Instead of looking at myself, I dismissed their comments as jealousy and immaturity. At the time, I didn't care what they said or how my alleged behavior impacted them. I accepted offers to dance while walking back from the restroom, and danced several songs while my date watched me from the bar. I also took telephone numbers on folded napkins when my date was away getting me a drink. I did these things on a regular basis, without considering what these actions meant. They were just a part of who I was. My disrespectful actions led to the demise of several of my relationships. I was only concerned about myself. There were deeper issues underneath.

On the surface I was an attractive and smart woman who had it "going on." Yet, internally, I didn't respect myself or men. I was trying to fill an empty well with attention from everyone. With my ego in charge and my emotions disconnected, I created a lot of suffering for myself and others. This was my baggage.

Now, at age forty-five, with my past behind me, I look back over the years and take full responsibility for the life I lived. I recognize my inappropriate actions and the insecurities that led me to select men who were not good for me, despite the red flags. Because I failed to set high standards for myself, I created much of my own pain.

Today, I see things much more clearly. I say, "No thank you," to men and situations that aren't good for me. I have rid myself of many of the old thoughts and ways and I make it a point to keep company with positive, fun, and spiritual people. I live a virtually drama-free life most of the time.

When you look in the mirror and ask yourself honest questions while admitting the truth, breakthroughs can occur. Only you can change your situation. Until you decide to change, however, you will repeat the same behaviors, make the same mistakes, and end up in similar situations. The definition of insanity is doing the same thing over and over and expecting a different result. I can relate, and perhaps you can, too.

Chapter 9

Letting Go (When Love Is Gone)

Rhonda

I know many of you remember the classic song "Neither One of Us" by Gladys Knight and the Pips. For those of you who need a reminder, please go to YouTube and pull it up, really listen to the words of that song, and hear what she is saying. Anyone and everyone who has ever been married and divorced or loved someone who they had to let go of will be moved by this famous song. Gladys hit every single point in this farewell message. This chapter is about learning to let go when love is gone.

Letting go of someone you love is one of life's most painful experiences, but staying with someone who no longer loves you, or staying in an empty, disrespectful, unfulfilling relationship is worse and it's futile. When love is gone, it's gone. It's like Humpty Dumpty falling from the wall and cracking into a million pieces; all the king's horses and all the king's men cannot put it together again. It's like a crystal glass shattering on the floor; trying to put it together will only result in cuts and pain becuse it can't be fixed. Love is the glue, cement, and the nails that keep a relationship together; without it there is no relationship. It's two holographic images of people appearing as a couple.

Typically, when love is gone and people remain in the relationship, both partners are emotionally numb, simply existing together every day until something gives, or until someone cheats. More often than not, the broken couple is waiting on that moment when they can exit without hurting the other too much or without losing too much, and far too many are "waiting till the kids grow up" or until ________________________________ (fill in the blank), as they allow the minutes, hours, days and years of their lives to slip through their hands.

It's always one person wanting it to end it and the other holding on for dear life. Rarely are two people in agreement when it's time to go. Rarely does it happen when both the wife and husband sit down and say, "You know, I think we should divorce and seek our happiness, we haven't been happy for years and we both deserve that," and the wife Jane says, "You know Tom, I think you are right, I've been thinking the same thing for quite some time now, so let's sort this thing out, and by the way have you given any thought to what you would like to keep as far as furnishings, jewelry and cars go? What's a fair amount of child support? And how should we divide up these bills? Do you want Jason and Sabrina every weekend or every other weekend? I just want to be fair in everything. And considering our decision, we will just sleep in separate rooms and make the best of it until the divorce is final."

Closing out the discussion, Tom says, "I'm so glad we see eye to eye on this! We both know it will be hard but the love and respect for each other will carry us through."

Jane says, "Absolutely, so let's schedule to meet with the lawyer on Wednesday. How does that work for your schedule Tom?"

Clicking my heels together three times and here we are back in the real world.

I interviewed a man named Tommy, who shared with me the story about his best friend, a guy whose marriage story had to be told here. I will call the couple "Mr. and Mrs. Stinson." They have been married for fourteen years. The Stinsons have been unhappy for most of their marriage; they were happy the first few years, but after that it's been all downhill. Mrs. Stinson is a medical professional, educated, and according to Tommy, "a nice looking woman." Her husband is a blue-collar worker who makes good money in his field. The Stinsons drive nice cars, live in a comfortable suburban home in Georgia, and from the outside looking in, they appear like a perfectly matched couple living the American dream.

Eventually Mrs. Stinson found out that her husband had been having an affair for a few months (this would be his third affair). One day, Mrs. Stinson learned that her husband and his new girlfriend were at a local restaurant having lunch. Just as the unsuspecting couple was coming out of the restaurant, she pulled up in her car and saw him kiss the woman good-bye as she was getting in her car. The wife then backed up her car, pressed on the gas as if entering the highway, and began ramming full speed into the woman's car, repeatedly crashing into it, apparently trying to crush her alive. No one could believe what was happening. Seeing that the situation was out of control, the girlfriend somehow jumped out of her car and ran back into the restaurant, understandably scared for her very life!

The wife and husband, in the meantime, were engaged in a full-blown fight out in public. She was crying and screaming hysterically and appeared to have taken leave of her senses and the husband was in a state of shock, doing his best to control her by gripping her in a bear hug. The girlfriend called the police from inside the restaurant and after it was all said and done, witness testimony given and the observation of damage done to car, the wife was hauled off to jail. The girlfriend pressed charges against Mrs. Stinson and this case went to court. The wife was sentenced to jail and she may very well lose her professional license.

Three affairs (which should have been a red flag or at

least an indication of something wrong), years of apparent misery for both, no ability to communicate through the issues, no one wanting to be the first to call it quits, no respectable break up, and now jail time and legal fees for the wife who lost her mind trying to hold on when love was gone.

I had an update by my friend who informed me recently that the divorce is now final between the Stinsons. The former husband and his "other woman" are now a happy couple. The wife has a felony record and is now starting over—the hard way.

Then there is the story about the dentist in Texas who discovered her husband was cheating and decided to run him over with her car as he and his mistress left their hotel room. She chose to do this, however, with their stepdaughter in the car. This philandering husband wasn't as lucky as Mr. Stinson: she killed him. The stepdaughter testified against her and wifey is serving twenty years in the big house for the crime. Her career, her life as she knew it, and everything she worked for her whole life is over. Letting go before losing her mind would have served her better.

And how about that Jodi Arias, who was convicted of killing her boyfriend once she assumed he had moved on and possibly found someone else? How is that for control? As this book goes to press, she was facing a sentence of either death, or life in prison with a chance of release after twenty-five years.

Yes, there are countless stories about jealous and crazy men doing the same thing to their significant others, beating up the other man or killing girlfriends, or wives and even innocent children because she wanted out of the marriage or relationship. And the question is, why? Is it really worth it? What are we holding onto when it gets this bad? The house, the cars, the bank account? The image of "the intact loving family"? What about our children do we not believe that they see our lack of joy, our unhappiness and hear our arguing? Are we tolerating abuse, disrespect and or unhappiness just to be able to say, "I have a man or I am married?"

Okay so maybe you haven't plotted to stab, shoot or kill your ex-boyfriend or husband, but most women reading this have done something semi-crazy, if not full blown insane, when trying to get a lover back. And those are the people this chapter is directed to. It's critical to understand, when love, trust and passion are gone, and when a man no longer wants you in his life, all the calls, crazy acts, begging, letter-writing and crying in the world, won't save it or make him want you back. It doesn't matter how good sex was, and how many times he said he loved you or how much you loved him. All of that is in the past now. Letting go of him and the relationship is your only option. Trust me, I know this to be a fact!

Another couple I know is in the midst of a marriage on its last legs. They have been married for over two decades, with the last five years being particularly sexless, loveless, and disconnected. Both have gained over thirty pounds in the past couple of years, and their misery is palpable. They go to work, come home, talk about the kids, sometimes go out to have dinner as a family, sometimes with friends, or they come home, sit in front of the television and vegetate. He pays the bills. They drive hot new Infiniti and Lexus vehicles with all maintenance done on schedule. The lawn in front of their 7,000-square-foot home is manicured to perfection, not a blade of grass out of place.

He claims he hasn't had sex in months, saying, "I've been without it for such long periods in my marriage, that I didn't think my penis worked! I was convinced I couldn't get excited or feel for anyone in the normal sense of the word anymore." Affairs became his thing, his way of finding connection. Hers was shopping and other secretive ventures that kept her out late nights on occasion. Over the history of their marriage, they attempted to talk through some things and it always resulted in the blame game: "It's your fault!" "No. it's your fault!" then days of silence and daily living that would bore a monk. That is their life. He isn't feeling sexually pleased, or appreciated as the provider for the family. And she isn't feeling heard or respected. Each twenty-four hour period, the cycle continues. Nights turn into days, and days into nights. Years come and go.

When asked why he doesn't leave, he says, "I just wanted to try and keep the family intact, trying to do what's right from a religious perspective. Honestly, the other side of that is I've been paralyzed by the fear of leaving. I didn't want to abandon my children, I wanted to see both of my kids through college. I have one left at home and I was trying to hang in their till he went off to school in a couple of years. Also, financially I've accumulated so much and I am responsible for so much, it was just easier to stay and be miserable."

Behind the snazzy maple and beveled-glass double door, they argue more often than not and when they aren't arguing, they aren't speaking at all, walking around their suburban mini-mansion on eggshells, trying to keep the peace for a day or two until the next fiery moment when the shit hits the fan.

We can spend our entire lives just barely holding on to a dead relationship or we can opt for better: to thrive, be happy, and live. It's our hour glass of time. We have to be able to discern when it's time to go. There are always signs the marriage or relationship is in trouble. If we act on those signs early we might be able to save it. Kind of like getting pre-screened for cancer, the earlier it's detected, the better the odds. The opposite is also true; if we wait to see a doctor until we are in stage four or five cancer, our odds of surviving decrease dramatically.

We never want to be the woman being dragged out of the house, holding on to his ankles, begging him to stay, while he and the next woman are walking into the crib—think *Diary of a Mad Black Woman*, opening scenes. There are always signs that it's over, we just chose to ignore them.

Question to consider if you did, in fact, save your marriage or relationship: If hypothetically speaking you somehow are able to keep your broken relationship intact, or get your man back, do you think love will magically return and all of your issues will suddenly go away?

To those who have actually held on for a few more years, or fought to keep the status quo (yes, I was that woman, too), you know that it doesn't get better; you are prolonging the inevitable, wasting a few more precious months and years. Barring divine intervention, amazing couple's therapy with the likes of a Dr. Phil, and two people who want the marriage to work and who are willing to let go of ego to surrender to what's best for the marriage, it never gets better. It only gets worse.

I've been the girl who went to her ex's house and "keyed the car" (years ago) because I knew he was in the house with another woman. I've been the brokenhearted and guilt-ridden woman who foolishly sent a letter to a man's wife, to let her know of my affair with her husband, because "I thought it was only right she knew." (By the way, she stayed and they are still living happily ever after—go figure.) I've also been the woman, calling the other woman to find out if she was seeing my man, and saying bad things about him, thinking if I could make her not want him, then I could keep him with me. What I learned is that it just isn't so. When a man is ready to go, you are powerless.

So how do you let go? Here are some options:

Make a List. As Shanae Hall noted in her May 2012 *Huffington Post* article "Coming to Grips with Not Being In Love with Your Spouse Anymore," letting go means making a list of all the hurt, pain, disappointments, and reasons why you haven't been happy with that person. For instance: "he cheated on me, he disrespects me, he's abusive, he isn't a good parent, he doesn't provide and lacks ambition." Other possibilities might be: "we don't love each other anymore, we don't communicate well, we don't have success, we aren't good for each other, I am not attracted to him, I've outgrown our relationship, he isn't a good role model for our kids." Post your list on the walls in your home and office where you can see it. We need this list because without it, our mind plays tricks on us and all we remember are the good times. Our memories don't serve us well when we want someone back. It's about honesty. This list will remind us why we have to keep moving forward.

Read, listen and watch! Read self-help, relationship and spirituality books. Barnes and Noble and Amazon are your best friends during this time! Listen to motivational and inspirational podcasts (like on Oprah's website, and her Lifeclasses). Talk to people who have been through it, who have your best interest at heart, and who can motivate you.

Pray, mediate and journal. Prayer and meditation are key. Without prayer, I don't know where I would be. It's that connection to Spirit that restores faith that you can make it through. Writing in your journal also is a big help. When you can't tell it to someone, writing it down on paper is an excellent way of getting out what needs to be said without fear of being judged. This, too, has been a godsend for me.

Cry. Crying cleanses the soul. There is nothing like a good cry. You feel better, it releases emotions, and it's healing. Crying and feeling sad is normal after letting go of a loved one. The Neo Soul singer Lyfe Jennings sings about how crying, for your soul, is like washing your clothes—it's good and cleansing These are words of wisdom, no doubt. Give yourself time to grieve. Just don't stay there. Fight to get through it and to the other side to happiness.

Get busy living! Go to the gym or to the park, and walk, bike, or run often. Work on being sexy and healthy for *you*. Go out with friends, join social groups, go to church, go dancing (one of my favorites), go to concerts, and travel. Meet up with positive women who have been through what you are going through and understand. And delete his numbers so you won't drunk-call or text him, or call him on those lonely rainy nights. (*Lawd* knows I've done that, too!) Whatever you do, get moving, get out the house! Happiness awaits you!

Yes, letting go of someone we love is heartbreaking but not more heartbreaking than holding on when love is gone. We owe it to ourselves to let go. It's an act of strength, courage and bravery to accept *what is* and to move on after all the options have been exhausted. The saying, "This too shall pass," is true. All pain from broken relationships "passes" and eventually the heart does go on. No, it's not instantaneous, but it will pass. But you gotta do the work. You must stay focused and keep stepping back to look at the big picture. Your life, health and happiness depend on it. That is what self-love looks like and this is what opens the door to a much happier life alone, and eventually with someone else. Sometimes losing is winning but we can't see that till we get to the other side.

Chapter 10
Knowing Your Place

Shanae

Before there was *woman* there was *man*. God deemed him to be wise enough to have *"dominion over the fish of the sea, over the birds of the air, and over the cattle, over all the earth and over every creeping thing that creeps on the earth"* (Gen. 1:26; KJV). And then some time later God saw that Adam was lonely and said that it was not good for man to be alone. God trusted that the man he created, in his image, was capable of naming all life and tending to it. Yet, for some strange reason, women today don't trust men to name their pets let alone, tend to the broken coffee table (believe me, I feel the same way at times). Where has the trust gone?

If I learned one thing from my marriage and from all of my male friends, it's that our men still need that trust from their women (or, as they call it, support, affirmation, loyalty). The truth of the matter is that most women don't know what the hell it means to "be in your place." I used to feel my place was any emotion I expressed at that time—hurt, anger, frustration—usually all negative emotions. In my mind, I could say anything I wanted to say, the way I wanted to say it. I never saw my parents communicate in a respectful manner. If there was a problem in our house, no one talked, and then both of my parents went out every night until the next argument. This endless cycle continued until they broke up.

In addition to not knowing how to respectfully communicate with a man, particularly, when I was upset, I also didn't understand and couldn't relate to the burden that a man carries with him every day. Men carry the burden of being the primary breadwinner, knowing that their wife and kids are depending on them to make sure there is food on the table, and that the lights come on when they hit the light switch. My husband would always say, "You don't know how it feels to get up and go to work every morning knowing that there is someone there ready to take your job." I have heard this same statement from entertainers, pro-athletes, and corporate men. I always thought a man's life was easy. It is the woman who has to give birth, wash clothes, cook, clean, take care of the kids, take care of the man, and work. And when we're sick, there's rarely anyone to take care of us (this is still a fact). As a woman, I can't comprehend the worries and burdens of a man. I can't even begin to pretend. What I do know, however, is that men and women have very different ways of looking at the world and at each other.

Affirm

Affirming your man is important. My ex-husband used to say he got more affirmation in the streets than he did at home. I interpreted that to mean he received more compliments from girls on the streets than he did from me. I would immediately become defensive, and my response was always, "Well, those chicks don't live with you, so go get it from them!" He did. One of my male friends told me that affirming a man (e.g., "I'm so proud of you, baby," "Good job," "Thanks for taking caring of that today.") was just as important as having sex with him (hard to believe but apparently true). I then began to realize how insecure and needy men really were. Although they don't express it the way that women do, men want and need the same confidence-building words to come from their partners as women do.

A celebrity friend of mine was getting ready to shoot a pilot for a cable network that he wrote and produced. On the first day of the shoot, he sent me a text that said, "Wish me luck." I wrote back, "I would if I thought you needed it, but you are funny, talented, and extremely entertaining, so just go out there and be you." His response was, "You're right, thanks babe!" And then it hit me. No matter how much or how little a man makes, he needs that special someone to tell him, "I'm proud of you and you're special to me." Never assume that everyone tells him so he doesn't need to hear it from you, too. You must put positive energy into him. If you don't, someone else will.

Support

I used to think *support* meant believing in someone who didn't know whether to wind their butt or scratch their watch. In other words, supporting someone who was just lost. I never understood why Cory would yell and scream that I didn't support him. I thought, "Yeah, you're right. I will never support stupidity." What I didn't realize was that the things that seemed simple and small to me could have made a big difference in the way that he felt about himself and about me. To a man, "support me" means "believe in me and trust that I am capable of doing some things correctly." This may be as simple as letting him spend two hundred dollars trying to fix something that cost only thirty bucks to replace, but because he did it wrong the first two times it has become much more expensive. Or it may mean supporting his decision to quit his steady job, with a 401k and health benefits, in order to live out his dream of being an entrepreneur. I encountered both situations and both times I failed to be supportive in some way. One time my husband wanted to call an electrician out to change a fuse. The charge was about two hundred dollars. I went and bought the fuse for about ten dollars and changed it myself in three minutes. The problem was not that I did it myself. The problem was that when it was done I asked him, "Was that really too hard for you to do? You have all those muscles for nothing." I seemed to make a habit of proving to him that I didn't need him. This is where we, women, go wrong. Some of us don't know how to let a man be a man.

I made my man feel incapable. If something was broken, I tried to fix it before I paid someone to fix it. I am a very handy person, and it drove me crazy that he couldn't fix things or was too lazy to fix things around the house. Instead of nagging him about his inability to fix things, I could have handled it differently. I didn't have to add to his insecurities.

Sex

Next, but probably the most important to a man, is sex. So many of my married, male friends ask me what to do to get their wives to have sex with them more often, and without them always having to initiate it. I have a good friend who plays in the NFL who called me and said, "Shanae, what else can I do? I leave her notes in the fridge telling her I love her. I send gifts to the house while I'm away, but she still doesn't want to have sex with me." "Why do you think that she is going to have sex with you now?" I replied. "You said she didn't give you any before the baby or before the ring." "I thought she was holding out until we got married," he said. "I told you before you married her, most women who like to have sex don't just have sex every two months, waiting for the wedding day. It's all or nothing," I stated. He asked, "What should I do?" I replied, "You have to tell *her* like you're telling me."

I am not sure how some women expect to keep a happy home when their man can't get any relief at home. I mean that literally. I interviewed one of the managers at my bank. He said it had been eighteen months since he had intercourse with his wife. He lives with her and he sees her every day. How is that possible? Often sex with his woman is all it takes to change the entire course of a man's day or week. Giving your man sex is one of your roles as his woman, but don't do it out of duty. It makes a huge difference if you want it just as bad as he does, and if you initiate it. This will definitely be an ego-builder for him.

No Talking About Your Other Man to Your Guy

A common no-no that women seem to do all the time is to try to make their man jealous. Every time you mention another man's name or what he has done for you, you put doubt and insecurities in your man's head. And as sure as the day is long, all those insecurities will come back to haunt you. My friend Mark recently told me that when a woman complements another man in front of her man all he hears is *"she wants to have sex with him."* I hope that not all men are that insecure but I am starting to believe it's true. So watch what you say (unless you don't want to be with the guy anymore).

Know Your Role

It is important for you to know and understand your position in his life. Are you wifey, girlfriend, girlfriend on the side, or booty call? Once you know your role then you can decide to quit or stay on the team. If you decide to stay, you must view your current relationship title as a job title. With every job title, there are certain requirements and expectations that need to be met in order to keep your job. If you go above and beyond the call of duty, you are likely to be promoted. On the flip side, if you are only doing the bare minimum in order to get by, you can be putting yourself in position to be demoted (this applies to the man or the woman). In addition to knowing your job title and responsibilities, you must also know what you want from the man you're dealing with and know your worth. With a clear understanding of your job title and responsibilities, work to the best of your ability and within the parameters you have established. If that role doesn't work for you, or if you've determined through a re-evaluation of your worth and your standards that you deserve something better, you have the choice of moving on or communicating what you want and seeing if he is ready to accept the change. If not, then you absolutely must do what you have to do to bring yourself respect and joy. It is your time and your life.

Rhonda

As I mentioned earlier, in my former career, I was promoted every two or three years. I was on a very fast, professional track. My husband and I worked for the same corporation at that time, and, in fact, he started about a year before I did. I was driven. I studied the people, the corporation, and the various management positions with a goal to achieve each one, and I did exactly that. I tested well, interviewed well, and got the jobs I wanted. My husband was promoted only twice in the same fifteen-year period, whereas I was promoted seven or eight times. My ego soon became a huge obstacle in getting through the doors of our home. My position became who I was; I was defined by my job title. It was my greatest ally and my worst enemy. I was a former teen mom now making almost $100,000 a year. Talk about *ego*!

This is where I began to lose my place in my home. I forgot my role, and he began to suffer inside, which came out as anger and resentment. While I didn't understand any of this at the time, I most certainly do now.

I realize the title of this chapter, "Knowing Your Place," could be a bit offensive for some. Those who become offended are often the "independent women who don't need a man for nothing, except some of that good lovin'." But for the rest of us, grown enough to see that title and courageous enough to read through it, let's see what it means.

There were many times in my life when I didn't know my place. I hadn't considered my place nor had I been taught anything about it. I was independent, and I felt my place was to continuously remind men that I could do everything on my own. My place was to tell them "I don't need you," and to caution the man in my life that other men wanted me just as much as he did, if not more, and that he was expendable.

In my mind, I was "the bomb," so my behavior, words, and actions (or inaction) were a reflection of my attitude. The real problem was that deep down, I didn't believe in my own worth. I felt it necessary to make my man feel insecure, or less than a man, in order to feel better about myself. Out of ego, pain, insecurity, and sometimes dissatisfaction with his progress, I would chide him about any shortcomings he had and make him feel bad about them. Sometimes it was about him not making enough money, or not changing the oil in my car, or the sex that we had earlier in the day that lasted only ten seconds. My mouth and behavior were detrimental to some relationships. Back then, I felt it was my place to "check" my man and then demonstrate that whatever he could do, I could do better.

I didn't fully understand the importance of support, respect, or patience. I didn't know that you could still have a voice and be heard without being demeaning and disrespectful. I was a wife without training or skills. If you happen to have a good man who shows his love and devotion to you, maintains the household, and shows care for you and the family, then allow him to be a man. Thank him for bringing home his check, for spending time with the kids, for repairing things, for keeping the lights on, and for making sure there's food on the table. Women, if the goal is to have a solid, loving relationship with our men, then as women, we must learn our proverbial places, which may change according to the person, the situation, or the times. We must also understand how our actions, words, and reactions can impact our relationships. While being strong and humble yourself, respect him for getting his and doing the right thing. Remember, for those who deserve it, we need to show respect, support, and encouragement, as well as become that inspiration they so desire and need.

Chapter 11

Goodies Have Power, So Use Them Wisely

Shanae

I'm going to keep this chapter short, sweet, and to the point. From the beginning of time, a woman could get a man to wage war on an entire country if he wanted her bad enough. When my friend Johnny and I talked about the women he dated, he would say, "The only thing worse than her giving me some is giving me some." He finished his thought by saying, "Unless I really like you, after I get the goodies four or five times, what else do you have to offer?" And I thought, "He is just mean, that certainly can't be how all guys think." So one night I was talking to my boy Mark and he said, "The reality is that women are giving it up way too easily these days." My argument was that he's a celebrity, so that doesn't count. Girls feel like they're getting a once-in-a-lifetime opportunity to have sex with a star. I asked LT, who is a personal trainer, and he said the same thing. Women pay him to train them and then next thing you know, his clients end up butt naked on the leg extension machine.

This is mind-blowing to me. Why would I let a man into my body without some effort on his part to make me feel special? By special, I mean dinner, movies, gifts, money, spa treatments, quality time, and so on. All of this is at your fingertips when the man you are dating is trying to get some, and every man you talk to is trying to get some, even your "friends."

I will tell you from personal experience, holding out sucks. It can be very hard at times, especially if you don't already have someone on hand who has already earned the right to the goodies. Making your man spend money and time to get the goodies doesn't make you a gold digger, it makes you smart. Most men you encounter don't even deserve to smell the goods, much less try them. If you make a man wait long enough, he will give away his whole motivation. It normally only takes about three dates. Make a list of all the things you want your man to do or all the things you want to know about him before you give him some and stick to it. Your list will help you establish consistency, but you will see that being a woman with rules and standards can be a lonely plight. Trust me. It's eleven o'clock on Saturday night, and it's me, a bottle of wine, and my computer. Good luck!

Rhonda

I have been the woman who gave up the goodies too soon, sometimes with regret and a tinge of sadness. I gave up the goodies on the second date with my ex-husband, but, we fell in love and I married him. I've also tried the infamous three-month wait time, in another situation but that relationship still didn't last. So what is the right time frame? Who really knows? In truth, holding out on the goodies simply allows you time to get to know the man and see his character before giving him all of you. During this time, you will find out if he is thoughtful, kind, generous, fun, and if he really cares about you.

These are things that you should want to know. During the wait period, you may also want to ask the right questions and spend lots of quality time. Again, not all guys are going to be honest, but it's worth it to ask. Perhaps if you wait long enough, you will be able to determine if he is even worthy of being in your space. In addition, you will have shown respect for yourself, causing him to respect you even more. I didn't say he would like it, but you may find the more you control the desire, the better things will be in the long run. I can personally attest to this!

Part Three

Confidence is Key

Chapter 12

Finding Yourself

Shanae

The alarm clock went off, as it usually did in the morning, the sun just coming up over the horizon. On this particular day, however, I didn't hit the snooze button for a few more minutes of sleep or jump out of bed and into my daily routine. I stayed awake and let the music on the radio play as I lay still. A song by the gospel great Marvin Sapp started playing, and I kept my eyes closed as he began to sing, "I Never Would Have Made It Without You."

Today I didn't just hear the music; I also listened to the words and the meaning in the lyrics, really taking them in. They began to resonate with me. Marvin sang about God and how he is always there with and for him. How he would not or could not have made it without him, how he would have lost it all. Through the tests and the trying times, the Lord is always there and no matter the difficulty, we come out better—with strength and wisdom.

And through my closed eyes, tears began to fall, down my cheeks and onto my pillow. Those words hit me at the core of my being, and at that very moment, I realized it was time for me to grow up. Not in age, but in my emotional state. I had three small children, and my soon-to-be ex-husband was coming and going as he pleased.

Yet, I had no idea how to take the first step. I was so shattered. My perfect life was coming to an end right before my eyes. The Bible says, *"Train up a child in the way he should go and when he is old he will not depart from it"* (Proverbs 22:6; KJV). The first thing I did was to get down on my knees and pray. I told God I would probably be there every day and several times throughout the day because I was lost. Because I had been through so much, I knew my first step would be to learn how to love myself again.

It sounds like something that would be automatic, but when you have been in a verbally or physically abusive relationship, your self-esteem and confidence are shot to hell. The first thing that I had to do was learn to love myself in my own skin. I had spent the last six years of my life pregnant, breast-feeding, being a stay-at-home mom and entrepreneur. Trust me when I say neither my body nor my mental state was on point. I was a physical and psychological mess.

I am 5'4" tall, and when I gave birth to my last child, I weighed two hundred pounds. The first call I made was to a personal trainer to get back in shape. I found a former Ms. Georgia bodybuilder to help me in my quest to find a healthier, sexier me, and I began working out four to six times a week. I didn't care if I just walked through my neighborhood; I was going to burn some extra calories. Once I got my weight down to one hundred and fifty-five pounds, I thought I would feel better, but I didn't. I looked in the mirror every day and thought that if my breasts were perkier, my butt was a little higher, and these stretch marks were gone, then I would be happy with myself.

One day my husband and I got into an argument. He pulled me over to the mirror, stood behind me, and said, "You still ain't shit. Look at you. No, really look at yourself (at this point, I started crying). You're a four, maybe a five on your best day. No one is going to want you. Oh, by the way, I'm seeing other people, so you can't say that I didn't tell you," and he walked out of the bedroom.

I cried for a few hours and I prayed. When I woke up, I realized that there are things that I couldn't change and that I needed to learn to love everything about myself, the good and the bad. But how could I do that? I had worked out consistently for eight months straight, I lost weight, and I cut my hair. I thought these things would make me whole, but still I was hollow.

Something told me to find a church. I had never had a church that I called home. That was my new goal. I found a place in Gainesville, Georgia, about thirty minutes from my house. This is where I began to transform from the inside out. I relied a hundred percent on God to heal me and to bring me through my turbulent times. My Bible studies became just as important to me as my workouts and my diet. My church body became my support system. I truly believe God puts people in your life for a reason, sometimes for a season, and sometimes for a lifetime.

Over the years, I have had the privilege of meeting some really amazing people, and my friend Mark is one such person. Our paths crossed at such an integral time in my life.

I remember walking backstage and seeing him. Our initial meeting was back in 1997, after his concert in Fresno when I was only eighteen, and he kicked me out because I was too young. Little did I know that our paths would cross again.

When we met again, Mark asked me how old I was now, and I told him I was twenty-seven. He told me I was all grown up now, and we both chuckled and nodded in agreement. As I mentioned earlier, we exchanged numbers and stayed in contact with each other over the next few months.

One December, I flew to Sacramento to watch him perform. A few of my girlfriends went with me. After the concert, he invited us to drive to San Francisco with him because he had a show there the next evening. My girls declined, so I went alone. Mark and I talked the entire ride to the Bay. He was a perfect gentleman. By the time we arrived at the hotel, it was two o'clock in the morning. I knew he was exhausted after working all day and then driving to the next gig, yet he stayed up with me and kept me company. We watched *New Jack City* until four o'clock when we fell asleep. He didn't try any funny business (to my surprise).

The following morning I had an eight o'clock meeting in Sacramento. At six, the alarm clock rang. Mark got up with me and made sure that the limo was there to pick me up and take me where I needed to go. It was freezing in San Francisco when I left, so Mark gave me his leather jacket and a small kiss on the cheek, and then he sent me on my way.

Several months had passed since my ex-husband and I had separated. He was living in California and the kids and I were still in Atlanta. He flew back home to visit the kids one weekend and saw the leather jacket Mark had given me in San Francisco. He said, "Whatever dude gave you this jacket is broke. Only a man that needs a loan would talk to you." At that moment, I realized that he was talking to a different Shanae. I responded in a nice, soft voice with a smirk on my face, "Is that so? That's Mark's jacket. This is not the same Shanae you left. Do you think he needs a loan?" I asked. Cory looked stunned for a second. Then he pulled it together and said, "You brought another man's jacket in my house?" (Hilarious!)

I can honestly say that over the next few months, Mark helped me become whole, and I love him for that. He was the first man who came into my life after a thirteen-year relationship. He was sweet and kind, and always said and did the right thing at the right time. The funny thing is that he didn't even know it. During my darkest hours, God sent me light to help create the woman that I am today.

When you ask God for help, you never know who or what he will put in your life that will give you all that you are missing. The next couple of years were dedicated to finding and becoming a better me. Lo and behold, I am now the confident and humble woman that can write this book and say, "I'm better because of the good Lord above."

In *A Course in Miracles,* Marianne Williamson (Lesson 193) says, "All things are lessons God would have me learn." Whether you believe this or not, just look back over your life and ask yourself what lessons you learned during the challenging times and whether you grew from any of them. I walked away from my old life, with the knowledge that I would be moving forward with a new me, and that was okay. I sincerely believed the scripture that said, *"With God, all things are possible"* (Matthew 19:26, KJV), and was confident that all things would be replaced. I now live every day to the absolute fullest.

Everyone has had something happen in their life that caused them to grow into their more mature self. I have yet to figure it out, however, if most people notice their breakthrough moment when it happens, or if they figure out what happened at a later date. For me, I believe it was the latter. As Elizabeth Lesser said:

> When we descend all the way down to the bottom of a loss, and dwell patiently, with an open heart, in the darkness and pain, we can bring back up with us the sweetness of life and the exhilaration of inner growth. When there is nothing left to lose, we find the true self—the self that is whole, the self that is enough, the self that no longer looks to others for definition, or completions, or anything but companionship on the journey (p. 56).

Like Lesser describes, this is where I was in life, waiting patiently for understanding and guidance, looking for a way out of the darkness of perpetual pain and into the light of hope and peace. If I recall correctly, this was the first time I truly realized I deserved better.

Once I experienced my breakthrough, I started making moves in a healthier direction. First, I had my attorney draw up divorce papers, and I personally handed them to Cory. Next, I sought counseling, which is where I learned to forgive him and to forgive myself. I had to restart my life. I truly had to start over and figure out what I wanted to be when I grew up. Since I was a kid, I had done what my boyfriend/husband wanted me to do. As a result,

I didn't finish my undergraduate degree from Fresno State that I had started years earlier. I did, however go to real estate school and got my real estate license. I always owned my own company, but if it required my leaving the house for too long or being around men, it was a problem. That was then.

Now I had an opportunity to make decisions where my husband's career and opinions about what I should do didn't come into play. I could do whatever I wanted. But what was that? What did I really want to do? I remember listening to the radio one day and Eddie Levert was talking about his music career. He talked about how he loved to sing and he would have performed for free. I thought, "Wow, that is amazing. What would I love to grow old doing?" Entertaining people in some way, shape, or form was the first thing that came to my mind, but I had to be the boss, too!

I thought I might be too old to start acting, but I could learn how to be a producer. This interest led me to California State University, Northridge, to pursue a Bachelor of Arts degree in Cinema and Television Arts. I accomplished this milestone in May 2010. Take a minute to ask yourself if you are doing what you want to do for the rest of your life. If the answer is yes, then keep doing it. If your answer is no, then find out what you really want to be and make it happen.

Don't worry, if you're doing what you love, the money will come.

Woman to Woman

Shanae

What are we really looking for? Are we getting it? Why do we stay when we are unhappy? Although some of the prior chapters may have come across as blunt or insensitive, I am simply trying to make a very clear point; we have to step up our game. I was watching a special on CNN a few days ago that asked why more men are reported as being happier than women. I laughed to myself and thought, "Well, let's see? Men get married and will still have a girlfriend, if they see fit, while we tend to kids, stay inside, lose ourselves in our families while they often live as if still single. That may have something to do with it, hmmm."

Male cheating statistics indicate that 70 percent of women are victims of adultery (http://www.infidelityman.com/statistics-on-men-cheating.php). Men still go out with their friends when they are in a relationship, while most women become permanent household fixtures. I have two girlfriends who entered into serious relationships as I was coming out of mine. Before they each had a man, we used to do girl weekends, go to the Essence Music Festival each year, and yearly one getaway trip just for the hell of it. It has been over three years since we have taken a trip together.

According to one of the guests on the CNN special, men tend to be healthier when they are married or in a stable relationship, whereas women tend to gain weight when they get a man. When a couple, with children, break up, the majority of the financial, emotional, and physical burden of the children falls on the mother. I wonder why men are happier?

Speaking woman to woman, we have to get past blaming each other and complaining about our failed marriages and bad relationships. We have to take a moment to evaluate where we are and how we got here. I have walked in both sets of shoes (married and single, broken and happy), and the one that feels the best is the pair I am wearing now. I know who I am—caring, gifted, and intelligent. I know my value now. I can see a red flag from a mile away. I understand that when things go astray we need someone to blame, but I think it's time we start with the woman in the mirror.

Rhonda

I think most of us would like to be married or with someone we really enjoy, and in a relationship where each partner can thrive, laugh, and love without reservation. If you are lucky enough to have that already, hold onto it, cherish and nurture it. Strive to bring out the best in yourself and your mate. If you are not in a good relationship, love yourself enough to leave the situation. Know your worth. You must do better, want better, and ask for better.

I have left many situations—jobs, friendships, and men—after determining that my mental, spiritual, and physical health were being compromised. Today I have little patience for situations that aren't good for me. It is not a race with a finish line. It is a journey toward enlightenment and improvement. The goal is self-growth and happiness.

I am so appreciative for lessons, special moments, spontaneous joy, time with good guys, friends, and family. In relationships, I listen more to what men say. I look them in the eye. I ask questions and I observe if their behavior matches. I give them the opportunity to be who they are and enough rope to hang themselves. The men in my life are of good character and have potential to be the "one". I now date with my eyes and ears open, and with all my senses on alert. I am enjoying single-hood much more today than I did when I didn't have direction. I have cleared the clutter and I am enjoying my life. Please read Maya Angelou's poem entitled *Phenomenal Woman;* it is a monumental tribute to all of us, even with our perceived flaws, insecurities, and past mistakes. Let it remind you of who you are today and every day.

Chapter 13

Knowing Your Worth

Rhonda

If you don't know your worth or you haven't realized your value as a woman, human being, and child of God, then the people you allow to occupy your time and your mind will keep your world unsteady and your mind in turmoil. Furthermore, they are less likely to add any value to your life. I'm not talking just about monetary value. I'm talking about intangible values: friendship, laughter, genuine care and concern, generosity, useful information, and kindness. Watch for people who bring chaos, deceit, drama, a lowered self-esteem, disappointment, stress, and any other maladies. We have to get to know ourselves first before we can attempt to know someone else and then hand them a set of our rules and standards. We really must *know* that we are worthy. We are worthy of better choices in men, friends, lifestyle, and health.

As a young woman, I hadn't a clue about whether I was beautiful or smart. I didn't really know what I was going to be, where I was going, or what I was going to do when I got there. I had two children by age seventeen, and I was a single parent from eighteen to twenty-three and several times after that. I had no real understanding of womanhood or self-respect. I was a victim of sexual violations by men whom my mother allowed into our home and into our lives. I am the product of a single mother with six children and numerous broken relationships (with trifling men). My mother suffered from lack of direction and very low self-esteem.

My body has been overweight most of my life. In fact, from the sixth grade through adulthood, I suffered from weight issues. By my early twenties, I had several stretch marks from my tender, teenage skin being stretched as my stomach grew with each baby. I gained between thirty and fifty pounds during both pregnancies. The small pouch in my lower stomach (yes, that dreadful pouch that men talk about us having) soon followed.

Shame was my shadow, and my continuous companion. Self-esteem was nowhere to be found. I was unaware of what it meant to have expectations of men and I was too afraid to say anything or to ask for anything. I feared that if I asked for something, they may not stay around or want me. After all, I had this ugly body, these two small children, and no other perceived or real assets (or so I thought). So instead of asking anything of the men in my life, I was the woman who needed to let men and others know I could manage it all. I became "successful" at earning good money, buying nice things, and living well.

I demonstrated that I was independent and strong and needed nothing from anyone. I would pay my own bills, buy my own gas, provide for my own children, and do everything myself. I might even pay *his* bills and buy *his* gas if he needed me to, just to show him I was nice and that I was there for him.

Later, I went through a marriage that lasted most of my adult life, and gave birth to two more children (one delivered by C-section). My body became even more scarred and disproportioned. My self-esteem was damaged even further, and my spirit seemed to be nonexistent. I was broken and I was in a broken marriage.

Then one day, I got a harsh wake-up call. There were many over the years, but this was the one that began the change for me. Late in my relationship with my ex-husband, I gained more weight than I realized. I was using the post-pregnancy weight excuse (you know, "this is baby fat, girl." Even if the child is eight or nine years old, we're still saying it's baby fat). Anyway, I was well past that excuse this time. In fact, I think my son was already six or seven, and I had gained and lost weight over the years. At this point, though, I was weighing in at about two hundred thirty pounds on a 5'7" frame. In the midst of an unrealized and undiagnosed depressed, sad, and lonely state, I didn't even see myself as overweight. Not until I saw pictures that were taken at various family events and my then husband began to say little things that really hurt. On so many occasions, I would ask him to take me somewhere, to a concert or out dancing, anywhere. Each and every time, he would say he was tired, or we didn't have the money, or use some other excuse. During the last days of our marriage, I heard about a concert that was coming to Atlanta. The artist was Jonathan Butler, someone we both loved. I bought tickets to the concert and asked him to take me. I pleaded with him to take me on a date, and he finally said okay. I was happy for a day in great anticipation of our date.

The next day, however, we passed each other in separate cars. He was leaving the house and I was headed toward the house. He pulled up next to me in his car and we both rolled down our windows. He then said he had decided he didn't want to go to the concert after all. "I just don't want to go with you," he said. I remember feeling so sad and lonely. We were in a relationship but there was no affection, quality time, or love. While I didn't realize the magnitude of the deterioration of myself or my relationship, I just knew something was terribly wrong and that we had a huge disconnect.

Months passed and I decided to do some things for myself. I decided to get into better physical shape. I've always exercised or at least had periods of my life when I would jog, go to the gym, and start a nutritious health plan. But this time was a little different. I knew I needed to do this to feel better inside and to look better outside. I always knew that being physically fit helped me feel better almost instantly. Jogging in the park, with my music in my ears, was always such a peaceful and motivating time. It gave me time alone to think, to cry, and to imagine without being interrupted by the kids, the phone, or men.

I also made an appointment for a consultation to get a tummy tuck with a well-known, board-certified, cosmetic surgeon in the Atlanta area. Yes, ladies, a tummy tuck! I figured it was time for me to have a drastic makeover. I went to my consultation, set everything up, and began working out while I awaited my surgery date. Almost two months went by, and I believe I lost ten pounds (not very much, but it was something), and it helped.

Just prior to my surgery, I noticed my husband kept getting calls from a woman he worked with at his part-time job. One day, I picked up the phone to return the call while he sat on the edge of the bed getting dressed. How is it that people who have professed to love us our entire lives can become so mean and cold toward us? I never figured that out. His face contorted and changed all kinds of ways while I dialed the number. He began yelling, "She is just a coworker. Why are you calling her?" Then he said, "You ain't shit; you're always f*cking up stuff." I called anyway. Not to cuss, scream, or challenge her, but to talk and find out why she kept calling, and to see if I could locate the truth. She never answered. I left a message and asked her to call me back. She never called back. Lord only knows what they were doing or why he felt it necessary to scream at the top of his lungs about a call I was making to a "coworker." I was, of course, troubled, hurt, fat, and miserable. Those days led up to my surgery and to the last days and months of our relationship (little did I know how close to the end we were). We still lived in the same house. And I still needed him to pick me up from the surgery center and help me make it through recovery.

I went into surgery and came out five hours later. My husband came to pick me up, and I was completely out of it. The drugs, the pain, the anesthesia, and the sheer magnitude of what I had just gone through had an enormous impact on me. I was out for the night. I was glad I did it, and I was excited about the change it was going to bring to my life. He was helpful but aloof. He did what was necessary to make sure I was okay, but there wasn't any love in the room or even the house, for that matter. I suffered post-surgery pain unlike anything I'd felt before. I had many sleepless nights because of the pain. To top it off, different areas of my incision didn't exactly heal like they were supposed to. But in time, with numerous follow-up visits and checkups, I eventually made it through.

The incision began to heal, but more importantly, so did my heart and spirit. Not because of the surgery so much, but because I began listening to and reading inspiring books, spiritual books, and praying a lot. I began to feel like I deserved better than a "so-so" situation and a "loveless" relationship. I also began to take an introspective look at myself. I began to ask myself questions like, "What are you doing?" "How did you let yourself go?" More importantly, "Why?" One of the most startling realizations I made was when I acknowledged my "loveless" relationship was not just with my husband, but also with myself.

As my body continued to heal, I slowly began to incorporate more exercise. I would get dressed with my support garments underneath my sweats, so that my wound would remain closed, and I began walking at the local park. First one mile, then one and a half (huffing and puffing along the way), then two, then two and a half, then three, and so on.

Eventually, after months of walking and walk-runs, I began jogging. At one point, I was up to five miles per day or every other day. It was exhilarating. My stomach still wasn't the picture perfect stomach I wanted at that time, but I could see a vast improvement. The C-section scar was gone, and a whole lot of the stretch marks and wrinkles were gone, too, as was the pouch.

My stomach was still puffy and big as far as I was concerned, but aesthetically, it looked a whole lot better, and I felt better. I continued exercising, reading, and progressing along my journey toward healing inside and out. Eventually, I moved into an apartment with my children. Shortly after my months of working out and gradual healing, I went into the office wearing some nice fitted jeans and a cute top. My ex-husband and I owned a small business together and shared an office. He was reaching for me like he wanted to touch me. He said, "Damn, you look good." I smiled and sat down. Then I gathered up the courage to ask him why he had been so distant over the past couple of years and why he never wanted to go out anymore. He hesitantly replied, "I just wasn't attracted to you anymore. You were overweight and I didn't want to be around you or touch you." He went on to say, "I know that sounds harsh, but it's the truth." Ladies, when I tell you I was stunned, I was stunned, speechless, and sick to my stomach. Here sat the guy who I virtually carried on my financial back during our marriage and post marriage; took on nice trips and vacations to the Bahamas, Las Vegas, and other places; helped to pay off his debt; and bought him nice gifts. This was the father of my children, mind you, who sat there and told me that the reason why he didn't feel like he could go out with me or make love to me was because I was too heavy. Well, I'll just be damned! How about that!

After I picked my lip up off the floor, I got up and walked out of the office. He, at this time, was all hugged up behind me, asking for some of my goodies. Imagine that?

I left the office that day knowing two things for sure. I would always do whatever it took to keep my physical health intact and that loving myself would be my new priority. I also knew that I would set a different standard for what and whom I would allow in my life.

I was angry and surprised at first, but then I regrouped and tried to look at it from all angles. I began asking myself a number of questions. Was he right to treat me this way for letting myself go? Should he have said something earlier? Should I have noticed earlier? How did I allow him and his broke-down situation into my life before and after the divorce? Was I needy? Did I do it for the kids? Most importantly, I asked myself where I should go from here. Let the liberation and change begin. I thought, and so it did.

Ladies, if you marry or find your mate and you are a size six or eight and he has a size thirty-four or thirty-six waist, both should try to stay that size. Even as time goes by, you should do whatever it takes to stay sexy for your mate and healthy for yourself. I felt sorry for myself, and I thought his comments were mean and selfish. But truthfully, I wasn't the beautiful, sexy, and passionate woman he had met years ago. I wasn't healthy or attractive on the inside or the outside. That doesn't mean you should subject yourself to mean comments or endure bad treatment, but try to maintain what is appealing to your man and to you.

Some of you may identify with my story, and others not. For those of you who do, I want you to know that I feel your pain. I also want you to know that although surgery was something I felt I needed and wanted to do to help me feel better about my body, that doesn't necessarily mean it's the remedy for you. You should also know that the surgery removed all of about five pounds from my stomach. The rest was up to me to lose through hard work, exercise, and eventually through changing my thinking and eating habits. These were by far the hardest weight obstacles to overcome, and I am still working through them. To date, I have lost about thirty-eight pounds and counting. I am still on my journey. I'm not on a diet but I'm participating in a lifestyle change. I now like myself well enough to at least do this for me.

I also practice daily spiritual guidance through books, podcasts, and meditations, thanks to Oprah's Spirit Channel, Eckhart Tolle, Marianne Williamson, and many other authors of memoirs and inspirational books, like Elizabeth Gilbert's *Eat, Pray, Love* (New York: Viking, 2006). It's not a once-in-a-while thing. I work out five to six days a week, and I read or meditate daily. To make a very long story short, I had to make an assessment of everything. It was time for self-healing, and a new direction. Self-worth, self-love, and self-appreciation are the starting points to setting standards and limits on what's acceptable in our lives with men.

Girlfriends, choose your own methods of healing and getting back your self-worth. Do and receive the things that bring you full circle, that give you joy and quiet time, whether that's church, spiritual books, friendships, exercise, prayer, or meditation. But by all means, get to a point in your life where you begin to understand how incredible you are. Once you get there, or begin the arduous journey, good things will begin to manifest slowly but surely in your life and your standards for the men in your life will change. I must warn you, it might mean more nights alone, and the quantity of men may be drastically reduced, but the quality of people drawn to you will be better and you will be happier. I guarantee it.

Shanae

Although my mom and I agree on a lot of things, I will say that it is hard for me to get mad at a man for not being attracted to a woman when she's out of shape. The reality is men are visual. So if you don't take care of yourself, it's hard for them to want to take care of you. That's a tough statement, but it is real. Entering into a relationship of any kind is a big decision, believe it or not. Whether it's a friendship or sexual relationship, emotions and trust must be part of that bond in order to make it work. Women and men are so different when it comes to what attracts us to a person of the opposite sex. Men are attracted to the physical and women to the emotional. Women are also a little more complicated than men. Men seem to have so many more options than women. As such, women seem to think they have to settle for whatever man is interested in them. Women, this is completely false. Yet, we have done this to ourselves. For so long we have not known or understood our true self-worth and potential.

How many women do you know who got married, had kids, and their bodies changed? The baddest chick in the world is never going to be the same after giving birth to a child. It's like having a bad car accident—you can get a whole new exterior done to fix the damage, but when you drive it, you're still going to hear a strange noise that wasn't there before. You can minimize the effect by eating right and working out, but your body will never be the same.

Now, how many men do you know who hate the fact that their wives are not built the same as they were when they got married? I know plenty that complain about their wives' bodies, the way they dress now, and so on. They feel that they have the right to cheat because their wives are no longer the women that they married. Most men would agree that women put themselves in a compromising position when they get out of shape. Okay, I'll go for that, but let's turn the tables for a minute. What if we married a man with money, a good job, savings, stability, and the promise of a great life and he goes *broke*? Is it our right to leave because he is not the same person or in the same financial position that he was when we met?

Don't be misled, men are attracted to the physical, but that doesn't mean he is going to marry you just because you're in shape or because you're pretty. Women are attracted to the thought of *security*. Women like knowing that if a bill needs to be paid, he is going to find a way to make that happen if something needs to be fixed, he can grab a tool box and get it done, or at least grab the phone and call someone who can fix it. Women also need to feel like a lady, which requires a real man.

For the men who are reading this, I am not saying that if something is broke and a woman can fix it without injury that we shouldn't, or that we should be 100 percent dependent on a man. That's not what I'm saying at all. What I am saying is that women need to know that you are their strength and that you can and will be everything they need. Why do you think that when a man buys a woman a nice purse, pays a bill, or the sex is off the chain, the first thing she does is tell her friends? It's to say, "Look, my man takes care of me. My man is a provider." Women thrive on the opportunity to brag on their men. Similarly, when a man is dating a fine woman, he wants all his friends to meet her. He is saying, "Look, I'm the man, I got a bad chick on my arm." Ladies, how you feel about yourself is a direct reflection of the man you choose to allow in your space. Let me give you an example. I have been told, more than once, that I am my biggest critic. I expect the world from myself. If I can give birth to three children, nurse all of them, and get back into shape after gaining forty pounds per child, why should I date a man who looks like he drinks lard through a straw? Let me help you out—I shouldn't! If a man doesn't care enough to take care of the only body that he's going to get, how is he going to take care of you?

If after having been married to an NFL player and living the good life, I could leave that man with nothing but some furniture, a prayer, and a dream to make something better of myself, certainly, I shouldn't settle for mediocrity. The man who wants to be in my life should have the same drive, will, discipline, and self-motivation to make a great life for his family and himself. I expect greatness from myself, from head to toe. From my pedicure to my relationship with God, I do everything to the best of my ability. The same applies to my man (I guess that's why I am single); settling is not an option. Don't get me wrong—I will have fun with guys that don't qualify; I just know that they won't ever be hubby. I do the same thing that guys do. I find out what position a man can play the best and line him up in that spot. There can only be one quarterback, so that person better have it all—smarts, agility, sexiness (that's my rule), and the ability to make me follow his lead. But as we all know, a great quarterback is the most sought-after person on the field, so you always need to have a backup, just in case he decides to resign and sign with another team, you'll be prepared.

Now it's your turn. Before deciding what you want in your man, let's see what you expect from yourself. Look around your house. What's on the wall? Do you have a degree, awards, or accolades? Is your house clean and organized? Look in your garage or car space. What's in there? Now look in the mirror. Are you in shape (or at least headed in the direction you want to go in)? Is your hair kept? Look at your hands and feet. Does it look like you have been scaling walls and kicking rocks? Go grab a bank statement. Are you straight or are you short every day, week, or month? How do you feel about yourself? Do you love the skin you're in—scars, stretch marks, and all? Or are you looking at someone else, wishing you were built like her, shaped like her, and with a man like hers? Do you love that you have another day here on earth, or are you asking God why He woke you up this morning?

You get the point; it's self-reflection time. Depending on your answers, you may be thinking, "My stuff is together, now I just need a partner." If this is your thought, good for you. He's on his way; just remember there is no need to settle. Now, for the greater majority of the women who need at least one or two personal repairs—let's talk. Whatever type of man you want is out there for you, but you have to get your stuff together. Take a moment and ask yourself two defining questions: "How can I enhance my own life and my own self-worth?" and "What is going to make me happy?" Once you figure that out, you can begin your journey to a great life.

Please understand that different men require different things. One man may want a size two, others like a fourteen; some like large breasts, some prefer big butts, some care about your educational achievements, and some won't. You have to get right for you. I had to step back and evaluate every aspect of my life. Numerous nights I asked myself what was wrong in my life. I had the big house on the hill, the nice cars, three beautiful children, and a gorgeous, NFL husband. What else could a woman want? Well, truth be told, I wanted a faithful husband who was nurturing, kind, and patient. I wanted to be able to get dressed and go out with my girls a couple times a month without my husband questioning my every move. I wanted to feel good about me. I wanted to be able to have my family over without having to plan it around the time when my husband wasn't home. I wanted to have a career that I loved and that I could see myself doing every day for the rest of my life.

I also wanted a career that didn't feel like work. I am a very social person and my husband felt I shouldn't interact with men without him being around. I realized that I was married to someone who was stifling my growth and who didn't treat me well. Once I came to this conclusion, I had to make a decision. Did I want to stay with this person I believed was stunting my growth? Or was I going to take a chance on myself and my belief that God would not forsake me?

Obviously, I chose the latter. I stepped out on faith and the desire to be happy. For the record, being single sucks. When I went through my reasons to leave and reasons to stay, I should have put sex on the reasons to stay list at least eight times. Other than that, I am so glad that I found out who I am and what I need in order to be happy. I am now prepared to bring happiness into my next relationship.

I have a very clear understanding of myself, what I need, what I want, what I expect from my partner, and what my partner should expect from me. Because I now know who I am and who I am not.

Chapter 14

Bonus Chapter

How to Make Him Want, Respect, and Keep You

Shanae and Rhonda

Today, we are still suffering and struggling to connect the dots. Even after *Act Like a Lady, Think Like a Man* and a host of other good books, the search for answers in how to make a relationship work seems to be a never-ending dilemma. The questions we all want to know the answer to is: How do we get the man? How do get him to respect us and commit? Then once we get that, we want to know how to get our man to do the things we want him to do like taking us dancing, keeping your car clean, and fixing things around the house.

We would like to build you up and tell you there is some magic dust, potions, or lotions to mesmerize that man you met at the comedy show or sports bar that will lead him straight into your arms in a trance and under your womanly control. We would also like to tell you that if you stay in shape, maintain your beauty by sipping on juice from the fountain of youth, go to church, stop drinking those Patron shots and cussing so much, he will adore you and remain faithful til death do you part. Some will lead you to believe that if you scavenge the earth to "find" a man, then learn to "understand" his messed up thoughts and mood swings, and follow the yellow brick road to Oz, you can get a man to do all those things and more. We too believe that there are steps to take in order to get the most from your man or a man you like, but it has nothing to do with mind games, or thinking like a guy. It has to do with something you already possess.

This is a three step process:

1. Getting a Man's Attention
2. Earning Your Man's Respect
3. Getting Him to Commit

Getting a Man's Attention

This one really isn't hard. Men are drawn to women. They are drawn to the natural physical us, meaning our clothes, smile, style, and bodies. Not rocket science stuff. But also to something that is almost unexplainable but very real, it's that thing called aura or energy. Chemistry also has something to do with it, and those things are derived from something deeper inside of you.

The truth is everything begins with you, the God in you and how much you recognize it. That becomes what you project into the world and to the men you meet. You, yes you, dear one, have all the power, all the tools and the magic to make it happen. It really has nothing to do with how much money you have in your account, what your size is, or how many kids you have. If you project confidence and self-love, it will show in how you walk, what you say, and how you say it. Men will see it the moment you walk through the door and open your mouth. In an instant, you will have their attention. This is always the first step.

I can't count how many times I have been in a place where women as well as men have come up to me and told me "you don't even recognize the light that is around you" or "your smile is infectious." That is a light that comes from a source greater than me. I just do me the only way I know how. When I am out, I dance like there's no tomorrow. I listen to my music and sing like I have a voice. When I talk to people, I listen intently and smile. My connection with those around me is genuine. I want them to know I hear and see them. I do this because I want to listen for the truth in them. The Bible also gives us insight to this phenomenon, as it says *"Do not let your adornment be merely outward-arranging the hair, wearing gold, or putting on fine apparel—rather let it be the hidden person of the heart, with the incorruptible beauty of a gentle and spirit, which is very precious in the sight of God."* (KJV, 1 Peter 3:3) Some ladies can walk in a room and time seems to stand still. People stop whatever they are doing and stare. It's not so much because of her outer beauty, because there are beautiful women everywhere. There is something more. She can be in the back corner of a room just talking and minding her business and before you know it, she is surrounded by men and women who find themselves sharing their whole lives and personal experiences and laughing with her til the sun comes up. Now I am not naïve here; we all know that physical beauty can draw people in but that intangible beauty is far more powerful. It is in the way she wears her skin. It is in her smile, the swagger of her hips, and the laughter she freely expresses. She lives in the very moment. Men are drawn to it everywhere she goes. Yet at the same time, she establishes that if you disrespect her by making some crass sexual innuendo, or off-color joke, she doesn't hesitate for a second to let a man know, the joke is on him and that he is in the presence of a woman. The boundaries are set instantly.

This "light" I speak of is in all of us. We had to find ours again after sorting through our baggage, and rising up from the ashes that was our previous lives. Getting a man's attention is easy, once you know who you are and who you are not. Keeping a man's attention is a matter of first having your standards in order so that you attract the kind of man you really want and by staying true to you. Being the same woman you presented when you first met him is what will likely keep him near.

Getting Your Man's Respect

Respect is something you establish from the beginning. Along the way in our book, we have given you examples of behavior that led to us disrespecting ourselves and that allowed men to follow suit. If you have cleared your baggage, visualized your man, asked the twelve questions, challenged yourself to take better care of your body, mind, and spirit, keeping a man's respect is a given.

You have control over what and who you allow in your life. Men will know it when you talk, they will hear it in the way you answer their questions and respond to their touch. Violators must be held accountable, instantly. Meaning if a guy comes up to you at a party, restaurant, or at the gym and even slightly insinuates something sexual, it is your job to tell him, "I don't know you, I find your comment offensive, and I would appreciate it if you didn't speak that way in my presence again." The conversation will continue with an apology from him and continued respectful conversation or he will head on out the door. Either way, you win. Respect is established. You have to remain consistent in your message throughout the relationship and in return, he will stay within those boundaries.

Getting Him to Commit

As you well know, this is our ultimate goal. We want commitment and monogamy. Well, at least most of us do. Getting the man to commit is not something in your power; that is his decision alone. Don't let anyone tell you anything different. You can't make a man marry you or commit. He has to want it. All you/we can do is be the best you, learn from lessons and follow the steps which we discussed in the previous chapters, the rest is left up to chemistry, timing, and God. Don't be fooled by any other advice.

The bottom line is: Men choose us. We on the other hand, choose who we allow in and under which conditions we accept him. A man will commit only when he is ready, willing, and able. You are powerless over that decision but are *powerful* over the rest of the process. I shared with you the story of Mr. Alabama in the single man's chapter. Well after months and months of the roller coaster ride of love that didn't work for me, I got off the ride and retreated. I re-established who I was, we had the straight talks, told him what I needed and wanted and that because he didn't offer that to me, I had to go. I told him I could no longer accept what he was giving. I changed my number and went about my life. He found me and connected with me again on Facebook, and demonstrated a whole other side of him that was humble, non-ego driven, and loving. He apologized for not appreciating me. Then a few months later, he asked me in a sweet nonchalant way, "When will you marry me?" Wow, this is coming from the guy who was "not looking for anything" and who was anti-commitment. Like I said, men choose us, we have to send the right message, know our worth, and set boundaries that give us our best advantage, then when they come ready, we get to say "yes" on terms that work for us and within guidelines that will ensure success and longevity. It always boils down to establishing what you need and want through direct communication, being honest, not settling for sub par answers or treatment and holding men accountable.

(FYI I told Mr. Alabama I would get back to him on the marriage question.)

Chapter 15

What Men Say (and Think) About Dating

Rhonda

Over the past four to five years, Shanae and I have spent countless hours interviewing hundreds of men about dating and relationships. In fact, almost every time I meet up with or talk to my male colleagues, friends, and sports acquaintances, the discussion of relationships and dating invariably comes up and I ask them questions. Thankfully, they oblige. In the summer of 2013, I sent out a survey of thirteen questions to random men of various ages and employment status. These were the questions that women seem to wonder about and discuss the most when it comes to dating. I was surprised how quickly the men responded and how open they were. This is unfiltered, straight from the man's mouth, though some of the names have been changed at their request. I am only able to give you a sampling of those responses due to space limitations. But anyway, here are some of the most refreshingly honest and most helpful ones that came in, in all their rawness and glory. Ladies take heed!

Bob Sumpter, Age Forty-Three, IT Professional (Not Real Name)

1) What is the first thing you notice when you see a woman, meaning what attracts you to her at "hello"?

   Her smile; that is her calling card.

2) When dating, who pays for what? First, second and third dates? And when, if ever, do you expect her to pay?

   I am a gentleman. I will pay for the dates but I will see how long before she offers. I can tell if I am being played or if she is truly in this for the long run. Also, you don't have to have a lot of money. Hell, if she can afford a girls night out, she can afford a dinner with and for me!

3) About sex, have you ever had a woman tell you to wait ninety days for sex? If so, did you wait? Does it matter how long you have to wait for it?

   I've never been asked to wait ninety days. I can't see that if I am really feeling her, human nature is a beast! And women want it just as bad as men. Women have told me I was going to get it (sex), before I said "hello." I just had to not fuck it up or be stupid or say dumb shit.

4) If a woman gives up sex the first date, or second date, do you feel differently about her? If not, or if so, why?

   If we have chemistry and it just happens effortlessly, that's kind of awesome. Everyone knows if it's a one-night stand or just the beginning of a sexual thing. Women should wait, unfair, but just do it. Real men do like to earn good women. These days women are taking value away from themselves. It's not just being quick to sex; they go to the highest bidder and give sex. So there is pussy for all to afford. They range from Golden Corral to Ruth's Chris Steakhouse—pussy for every budget.

5) Could you wait until your wedding day to have sex if you were really feeling a woman?

   I doubt it. I would get some. It does not mean I don't want her, but why play games? Sex is not going to make or break you if you are that strong of a couple. It's boring sex, bad finances, and terrible communication that make relationships fail (not when you have sex).

6) How do you feel about a woman asking you to pay a bill, or two or three, in the dating process? And how long should she wait before she asks you for money or to help her?

That just valued her. She is playing a game; doesn't have her money right. From time to time, everyone needs help. But you should be careful who you ask and when you ask. There is not a correct time, you will just know.

7) These days, do you still believe monogamy is possible? Can you really only be with one woman the rest of your life and be sexually fulfilled? What does she need to do that can ensure that (if anything).

   Damn good question! I want to be with one woman for the rest of my life. I hope she comes around. I don't know what she has to do. I guess sex me like a porn star, be my best friend, and push me to conquer the world and look like a movie star, i.e, Rhonda Frost or Nia Long.

8) What makes a happy marriage? Narrow it down to specific thoughts, like great sex, good communication, trust, or whatever you believe is key.

   All of those listed here plus taking care of yourself, exercise, nails and hair, nice perfume and white teeth.

9) Would you leave your spouse or girlfriend immediately if you found out she was cheating? Do you think she should leave you, too, if she found you were cheating?

This time I am trying to really be the real deal. I hope I give her everything she needs NOT to cheat and I hope she does the same for me. If she cheated on me, I really would have to sit down and see how much we have invested.

10) Do you believe men are still supposed to be providers for the family, or is that outdated thinking?

    No, men are supposed to provide, protect and plan, and "providing" may mean adding to the family income. Your lady might make more than you. Nia Long makes more than me but I would still be the man and add to her life. I will complement any woman's life. A lot of men are just sorry and try to live off of their lady and that is why so many men are locked down and make it hard for us good men.

11) What makes a woman wife material as opposed to just girlfriend status?

    Timing. A man has to be ready to settle down and give up the game. Age does not matter. There are forty- and fifty-year-old men who still try to play.

12) Can another woman make you cheat? Can she make you marry her, or make you fall in love?

    They can't make you—but sure can make it damn

hard not to cheat, or fall in love with her. She can say "marry me" or she is out. That does work if she has invested and the man is bullshitting.

13) On a scale of one to ten, with ten being "extremely important" how important is oral sex to you?

Oral sex is like investment banking: the more you give the more you get. BUT lawd please perfect your skills. I do it and expect her to as well. Rating is 9.8999

Maurice Johnson, Mid-Thirties, Teacher

1) What is the first thing you notice when you see a woman, meaning what attracts you to her at "hello"?

Initially it would be her appearance and how she is conducting herself. She can be dressed fine as wine (church women) but if her attitude and behavior is that of a **Love and Hip Hop Atlanta** ***woman, that renders her unapproachable to me.***

2) When dating, who pays for what? First, second and third dates? And when, if ever, do you expect her to pay?

It depends on what the festivities are. I have no problem with paying for food, entertainment, gas, etc., on a first date. But if we get to the second,

third, fourth, eighth date, and she ain't reaching in her purse, that is a sign that she is a gold-digger, and just along for the ride.

3) About sex, have you ever had a woman tell you to wait ninety days for sex? If so, did you wait? Does it matter how long you have to wait for it?

    I have no problem waiting ninety days. I have waited a year before. But I would have to be really into her. And plus there would have to be stipulations (laughing out loud).

4) If a woman gives up sex the first date, or second date, do you feel differently about her? If not, or if so, why?

    Hell naw, I wouldn't! Sometimes people just click like that. I am not like a lot of shallow ass dudes, who try to pass judgment on women. Now if she starts actin shady afterwards, then yeah. Imma start lookin' at her sideways out of my cockeyed eye (laughing out loud).

5) Could you wait until your wedding day to have sex if you were really feeling a woman?

    Hell yes I could wait. That would be the shortest engagement in the history of Engagementdom (laughing).

6) How do you feel about a woman asking you to pay a bill, or two or three. And how long should she wait before she asks you for money or to help.

   If she ain't my woman, or we don't know each other like that—she shouldn't be askin me for nothin'. Now if she is my baby, my girl, my boo thang, then she can get whatever I got. Can't go around giving every woman the privileges of a queen.

7) These days do you still believe monogamy is possible? Can you really only be with one woman the rest of your life and be sexually fulfilled? What does she need to do that can ensure that (if anything).

   Yes, I can be with one woman. The top three things she can do for me are: Be faithful, be freaky, and know how to be a woman to your man—or willing to learn.

8) What makes a happy marriage? Narrow it down to specific thoughts, like great sex, good communication, trust, or whatever you believe is key.

   Communication, trust, openness, faith, SEX, strength, and be spontaneous.

9) Would you leave your spouse or girlfriend immediately if you found out she was cheating? Do you

think she should leave you, too, if she found you were cheating?

I never cheated. And don't plan on it. It would depend if she confessed, or the Cheaters van, and Joey Greco, jumped out and caught her monkey ass red-handed (laughing).

10) Do you believe men are still supposed to be providers for the family or is that outdated thinking?

I think men should be the providers. But I also think that because of today's economy, that in order to run a household successfully, there has to be dual partnership in order to make it run smoothly.

11) What makes a woman wife material as opposed to just girlfriend status?

Her actions and behavior have to mirror that of a woman with wife attributes. As long as she is not your girlfriend, expecting to receive the benefits of a wife, you should be good.

12) Can another woman make you cheat? Can she make you marry her, or make you fall in love?

Not if I am already in a relationship with a woman. She might be able to arouse me, but that's about as far as it goes. I DO NOT CHEAT.

13) On a scale of one to ten, with ten being "extremely important," how important is oral sex to you?

Oral is a 1,000 to me—but a six to the overall relationship.

Laphonzo P., Age Twenty, College Student/ Part-Time Retail

1) What is the first thing you notice when you see a woman, meaning what attracts you to her at "hello"?

Style, hair, grammar, and body shape. These are the determining factors that I feel will attract me to a woman after the initial "hello."

2) When dating who pays for what? First, second, and third dates? And when, if ever, do you expect her to pay?

As the man, I feel that on the first few dates, I should pay, because that's the gentleman's honor. After the first few, I would say that the man and woman should alternate, or just go Dutch, depending on the circumstances of their relationship.

3) About sex, have you ever had a woman tell you to wait ninety days for sex? If so, did you wait? Does it matter how long you have to wait for it?

Yes, I have been told that before, depending on how sexually attracted I am to that person I will wait. If I am not physically attracted to that person then I will just move on, ain't nobody got time for that.

4) If a woman gives up sex the first date, or second date, do you feel differently about her? If not, or if so, why?

Not at all. We are human and have physical needs. As a bonus, sex can dictate the future of a relationship. If you aren't enjoying it, there is no need to continue on with the relationship.

5) Could you wait until your wedding day to have sex if you were really feeling a woman?

Absolutely not; as stated in my previous answer it is a major factor in determining the future of the relationship.

6) How do you feel about a woman asking you to pay a bill, or two or three, in the dating process. And how long should she wait before she asks you for money or to help her?

Depending on the circumstance, I would say anywhere from six months to a year. The type

of guy I am, if I feel that you are not up to par financially, I will not put myself in that position.

7) These days do you still believe monogamy is possible? Can you really only be with one woman the rest of your life and be sexually fulfilled? What does she need to do that can ensure that (if anything).

   Yes, through loyalty, honesty, and spontaneity. If a couple can keep it fresh and new it is very possible.

8) What makes a happy marriage? Narrow it down to specific thoughts, like great sex, good communication, trust, or whatever you believe is key.

   Honesty and open communication.

9) Would you leave your spouse or girlfriend immediately if you found out she was cheating? Do you think she should leave you, too, if she found you were cheating?

   Yes and yes. If I cheat, I've probably lost interest.

10) Do you believe men are still supposed to be providers for the family or is that outdated thinking?

    Outdated/old school. It is a new day and age. Women have more rights than they did in the fifties and sixties. Stay-at-home moms are a thing of the

past. With all the laws they have in place, women can provide just as easily as men.

11) What makes a woman wife material as opposed to just girlfriend status?

The person who is with me through good and bad, ups and downs, richer or poorer, and sickness and health—just like the vows—this is the key.

12) Can another woman make you cheat? Can she make you marry her, or make you fall in love?

No person can make you cheat. You are either with that person wholeheartedly or not at all. No one can force you to marry her. It is a decision that the person has to make and decide what is best for him. Anyone can make you fall in love with them according to what a person's needs and specific goals are, and if the person can fulfill them.

13) On a scale of one to ten, with ten being "extremely important," how important is oral sex to you?

Ten.

Jerry J, Age Fifty, Vice President, Fortune 100 Company

1) What is the first thing you notice when you see a woman, meaning what attracts you to her at "hello"?

   Her smile and her attire, meaning the way she carries herself from a fashion standpoint. Her smile reveals the soul; style reveals how much pride she has.

2) When dating who pays for what? First, second, and third dates? And when, if ever, do you expect her to pay?

   If I invite you out, I pay. If she invites me out, I expect that she will offer to pay, and that is the perception, but given the type of guy I am, I always pay.

3) About sex, have you ever had a woman tell you to wait ninety days for sex? If so, did you wait? Does it matter how long you have to wait for it?

   No, I have never had a woman ask me to wait ninety days. And yes, I would wait ninety days for the right woman.

4) If a woman gives up sex the first or second date, do you feel differently about her? If not, or if so, why?

Yes, I would feel differently about her. I would feel like she's done it before. I probably wouldn't have the same level of respect for her. I think the question should be qualified because the time frame between dates could be weeks or months and lot could have transpired in conversation and getting to know each other, so we have to consider that, too. But without that, I would look at her like she's the "fun girl." She would be perceived to be the "low hanging fruit."

5) Could you wait until your wedding day to have sex if you were really feeling a woman?

   If you are a single guy out there just "doing you", most guys won't be able to do it. But if you are a mature man looking for stability and the real things that matter—emotional, spiritual, mental, and otherwise—and the bond has been built, then yes.

6) How do you feel about a woman asking you to pay a bill, or two or three, in the dating process? And how long should she wait before she asks you for money or to help her?

   We should have already had sex, then it makes it okay for her to ask me for money. If I give you money, then it's likely we will be having sex. I'll pay a few months' rent for some good head. And if no sex is involved at the time she needs

money, then at least wait a month. Most brothers expect sex if he's giving money just so you know. But to be honest, I have helped women without any expectations at all. That's just who I am.

7) These days do you still believe monogamy is possible? Can you really only be with one woman the rest of your life and be sexually fulfilled? What does she need to do that can ensure that (if anything).

   I think it is possible and I think you can find fulfillment in one person but you gotta be creative in the relationship, and you have to be in touch with your partner. The act of making love is more of a spiritual thing for me, so I've got to have that connection with one person. Spreading yourself thin takes away from that. I can't replicate that with others added into the picture; it dilutes it. You become more animal-like than human.

8) What makes a happy marriage? Narrow it down to specific thoughts, like great sex, good communication, trust, or whatever you believe is key.

   Appreciation, empathy, sympathy, cooperation, collaboration, and compassion. If you lack compassion you can't capture the rest of these qualities. Compassion is sexy and intriguing. Good sex is a big part because it's the emotional connection to each other. When other things are lacking, like

financial or other areas, it (sex) keeps you close and connected. Trust is also key. I need to be able to trust you with my life and everything; without it, you have nothing.

9) Would you leave your spouse or girlfriend immediately if you found out she was cheating? Do you think she should leave you, too, if she found you were cheating?

No, not necessarily it would depend on what we had established. If there had been volatility already in the relationship, then maybe. But trust would certainly be damaged. And yes, she should leave me if I had intentions of cheating again or if I cheated again.

10) Do you believe men are still supposed to be providers for the family or is that outdated thinking?

In this day and age, with the volatility of the economy and the fact that men and women are now working outside the home, this is kind of outdated. I think the pressure of that ideology creates havoc for relationships. If it's needed, the woman should pull her weight. However most men from an ego standpoint believe being the provider is synonymous with being a man. I don't necessarily feel that way although I have always been in that role.

11) What makes a woman wife material as opposed to just girlfriend status?

    Stability. She can't be shaky (mentally, or otherwise), and she has to aspire to be more and have more in life, to continue to dream and grow. Trust is also a very big key. I have to know you have my best interest at heart and that you are working with me making good decisions.

12) Can another woman make you cheat? Make you marry her, or make you fall in love?

    No, I have to want to do it. That would have to be my mindset. Something I am putting out there.

13) On a scale of one to ten, with ten being "extremely important," how important is oral sex to you?

    A twelve; it would be nice to get that every time we have sex or even if we ain't having sex. Head game is important. Oral sex is the game-changer universally speaking.

Kevin P. Age, Forty-Four, Senior Business Development Manager in Telecommunications

1) What is the first thing you notice when you see a woman, meaning what attracts you to her at "hello"?

I notice her smile and character—how she presents herself.

2) When dating, who pays for what? First, second and third dates? And when, if ever, do you expect her to pay?

   When I ask a woman out on a date, I pay when I am asking (regardless of the number). It is okay for a woman to treat after she is comfortable or it is becoming more serious. A man likes to be treated, sometimes as a reminder that she finds him attractive and interesting.

3) About sex, have you ever had a woman tell you to wait ninety days for sex? If so, did you wait? Does it matter how long you have to wait for it?

   I never had a woman tell me a number of days; however, I have had women tell me to wait and when it felt right, it did not matter how long it took to have sex.

4) If a woman gives up sex the first date, or second date, do you feel differently about her? If not, or if so, why?

   There is something to waiting for sex, and I believe it's special to do, but if a woman has sex early it doesn't matter unless she is only looking for sex—and there are woman out there like that.

5) Could you wait until your wedding day to have sex if you were really feeling a woman?

   No.

6) How do you feel about a woman asking you to pay a bill, or two or three, in the dating process? And how long should she wait before she asks you for money or to help her?

   I do not believe anyone should ask to have a bill paid, male or female. It becomes prostitution to me if there is a "play to pay" and you will get sex or farther in the relationship; but a man can pay if he is feeling a woman and he knows she is struggling financially. Bill-paying should come if there is a future. Otherwise, it becomes an expensive vetting process to find your true love.

7) These days do you still believe monogamy is possible? Can you really only be with one woman the rest of your life and be sexually fulfilled? What does she need to do that can ensure that, if anything?

   Yes. She needs to show appreciation and respect outside the bedroom and a sexual fireball in the bedroom.

8) What makes a happy marriage? Narrow it down to specific thoughts, like great sex, good communication, trust, or whatever you believe is key.

   A happy marriage requires mutual respect, admiration, and appreciation for one another. The sex will be intense every time as long as you appreciate your spouse.

9) Would you leave your spouse or girlfriend immediately if you found out she was cheating? Do you think she should leave you, too, if she found you were cheating

   Yes to both.

10) Do you believe men are still supposed to be providers for the family or is that outdated thinking?

    I believe men should lead their families by following God's word and his purpose for his life. If he does that, he will be an extraordinary provider of whatever his family requires and, by default, he will be a provider with a helpmate.

11) What makes a woman wife material as opposed to just girlfriend status?

    A woman becomes wife status when she stands above all others in your life. She's genuinely

supportive. She motivates you and makes you feel as if there isn't a better man than you.

12) Can another woman make you cheat (if you are in a relationship)?

    Another woman can't make you cheat. If a man cheats (real man) it's his woman that may be the centerpiece or unresolved issues.

13) Can a woman make you marry her, or make you fall in love?

    A woman can make you fall in love, but you would marry her if you believe she's the one God has for you.

14) On a scale of one to ten, with ten being "extremely important," how important is oral sex to you?

    10 ++++.

Marshall Cullins AKA Milk, Age Thirty-Seven (Happily Married Now but Was a Big Time Dater/Player), Poet, Writer, Philosopher

1) What is the first thing you notice when you see a woman, meaning what attracts you to her at "hello"?

    Her body, face, smile, and energy.

2) When dating who pays for what? First, second, and third dates? And when, if ever, do you expect her to pay?

   If I ask to go out I'll pay but I love when a woman is willing to pay; it shows she's self-sufficient.

3) About sex, have you ever had a woman tell you to wait ninety days for sex? If so, did you wait? Does it matter how long you have to wait for it?

   No I've never been asked to wait, but I could if I'm feeling her. I have to decide if she is worth the wait. And, no, it doesn't matter because time doesn't change my outlook on what I know I'm going to get or deserve.

4) If a woman gives up sex the first date, or second date, do you feel differently about her? If not, or if so, why?

   It depends on the vibe we giving each other. And how far she goes sexual the first time if she's using all the tricks in the book I might. But if she's still classy with it more than likely I won't feel differently.

5) Could you wait until your wedding day to have sex if you were really feeling a woman?

   I say NO but then again, if I was up in age MAYBE yes.

6) How do you feel about a woman asking you to pay a bill, or two or three, in the dating process. And how long should she wait before she asks you for money or to help her?

   If I have to pay bills before we move in together I feel like you can't hold your own. It's nothing wrong if you need help sometimes but if I'm picking up bills every month that's a problem. It'll make me think: What were you doing before you met me to take care of these bills?

7) These days, do you still believe monogamy is possible? Can you really only be with one woman the rest of your life and be sexually fulfilled? What does she need to do that can ensure that (if anything)?

   Yes and yes. Just stay sexy, be sexually spontaneous, and keep in mind for every one man there's three or four women. It's hard, very hard, but it can be done. Just know that men want to be treated special also.

8) What makes a happy marriage? Narrow it down to specific thoughts, like great sex, good communication, trust or whatever you believe is key.

   No outside input from people in unhealthy relationships, or people who don't have anybody at all. You need friendship, great sex and both

people have to be on the same financial level or path. Then you must have trust, honesty, communication and laughter. Last, you have to keep going out with each other—dinner, movies, lounge, Vegas—you have to enjoy each other. FYI, when I say you both have to be on the same financial level, I mean you have to have a clear understanding on what needs to be paid and who pays what; also, what goals you have. If she's a spender and you're a saver it's not going to work unless you get on the same page.

9) Would you leave your spouse or girlfriend immediately if you found out she was cheating? Do you think she should leave you, too, if she found you were cheating?

   YES! No. As a side note, from the time you start a relationship, men think, "She's mine and I have that on lock," and most women think, "He's mine," but she knows most men are weak.

10) Do you believe men are still supposed to be the providers for the family or is that outdated thinking?

   Yes and no. If you struggle and you want to really win or provide a good foundation for the family, sometimes it takes two incomes. But if you are well off, why would you want your wife to work? She

can hold down the house and kids, most men would want that. But on the flip side, if the kids are older, I want a women to take some of this money and build an empire, so she should be doing something. It's unattractive for women not to make moves.

11) What makes a woman wife material as opposed to just girlfriend status?

    Be special, be different. Have layers to your personality. Always make me feel like I never figure you out completely.

12) Can another woman make you cheat? Can she make you marry her, or make you fall in love?

    No, it's just like crack; you have to stay away from it (laughing)! Only thing I can say is don't put yourself in a situation where you have to decide. It can only happen if you are already cheating in your mind or open to it.

13) On a scale of one to ten with ten being "extremely important," how important is oral sex is to you?

    Infinity.

Ladies, these men shared invaluable information in their responses that could be useful as we go about our dating and relationship lives. Whether you are open to oral sex, practice the "ninety-day day rule," or ever plan to get married, what I know for sure is it's up to us to continue to ask the right questions, take heed of what men say, and watch what they do. We are responsible for our bodies, time, and decisions, and for establishing boundaries for our relationship lives. We have to decide if men's answers to our dating questions (and their actions) work for us. But at least now, you have a sampling of what men say (and think) about dating.

Chapter 16

At the End of the Day

Shanae

At the end of the day, I found the strength to leave, the wisdom to do better, the courage to expect more of myself and my partner, the fortitude to step out on my own two feet and to believe in myself and to trust in God. I hope that every person who reads this book will find something that he or she can use to improve his or her life, relationships, and self-esteem. At the very least I pray that it will serve as a motivation for you to want more out of life. I hope that you were able to laugh, relate, and maybe shed a tear while reading *Why Do I Have to Think Like a Man?* It was very therapeutic for me to write. Many of the stories told in this book I told for the first time. I want to thank all the readers for becoming a part of my story. I leave you with this poem written by my grandmother:

Lost
Once you took my breath away, lost in your embrace.
It was then that I couldn't wait, to hear your
voice and see your face.

We've now become tied in a web too tangled and too deep.
You've grown into my flesh, even in our dreams we meet.
I go, you're there, I stay, you're here.
I rise, you're up, I sit, you're down.
I look into the mirror, I see your face,
I lift my hand, you place
Your moods control my feelings, your presence without end.
You no longer care how I look, only that I am
You have become me or am I you?
I can't separate between the two
I must untie, unshackle, and undo, to find the me I lost in you.

—Bonnie White

Rhonda

At the end of the day, once I got my standards right, things changed. Primarily, I liked me a whole lot better. I learned to trust my intuition and feelings. My spirit settled and I found more peace. The men I speak about in this book changed toward me as well. I began to get more calls, e-mails and texts saying, *"I miss everything about you, I would like to see you, please call me,"* and asking, *"Why can't I reach you?"* It never fails, ladies, as long as you are going along with the program, accepting whatever and being nonconfrontational, the relationship works "fine." Then when you say *no more* and refuse the status quo and sub-par treatment, suddenly you get their attention. They either step up or they bounce. It is predictable, humorous, and reassuring all at the same time to know, at the end of the day, we have what it takes to turn it around.

Throughout history, women have overcome great odds in many areas, and they have demonstrated undying strength and incomparable accomplishments. Whether it was Harriet Tubman leading hundreds of slaves to freedom through treacherous enemy territory, women fighting and winning the right to vote, African American women like Madam C.J. Walker, who revolutionized the hair care and cosmetics industries, or women like former First Lady, Hillary Clinton, running for the highest political office in the land, our great minds and profound power are evident. Because of our strength and unquestionable determination, we, women, have the ability to stand on our own merits and use our own thinking process to relate better.

No one book, therapy session, spiritual enlightenment meeting, epiphany, or "aha moment" is going to change everything in your life or help you find and keep Mr. Right. We can only wish it were that simple. However, a combination of some or all of these very helpful tools, coupled with your inner, intuitive, spirit serving as your guide, will help you discover how to better navigate your way through the dating and relationship maze on a higher level. If you set some standards for what you want and need from your man and stick to them, eventually you will weed out the men who do not have your best interests at heart and recognize those who do. Take the time to look in the mirror. Accept yourself where you are and then evaluate what you need to do to get to where you want to be with yourself, in your relationships and in life in general.

The old labels made by men like "gold digger," "bitch," and "independent woman" no longer have to apply as stated. The double standards men set, where they can sleep with as many women as they want and be given "props," or sleep with women without so much as buying them a bag of groceries or a tank of gas, need to end. At minimum, we should stop and think about it and challenge it. Remember, any woman can get a man to lie down with her any day of the week, but how many of us feel respected or empowered the next day or later that night? How many of us wake up and say to ourselves, "No matter how it goes, I am okay. I got more than I wanted or needed out of the situation." If 50 percent of marriages end in divorce every year, how many dating relationships end each year? We won't even mention the one-night stands, so give yourself a fighting chance at something good and meaningful. Give yourself every advantage at better dating. As you go on about this wonderful thing called life, explore all the options and tools available to you (wise counsel, spiritual teachings, the Bible, your parents, lessons), to uplift and sustain you. Take care of your body, mind, and spirit and welcome the man or men who will do the same. Finally, *thinking like a lady* means, staying conscious, being honest, removing blinders, setting standards, connecting to your source, and knowing who you are at all times. You already possess all that you need to get where you are trying to go, believe that! You are a Phenomenal Woman, read Maya's poem again to remind yourself.

References

Brett, Jill E. "Not Tonight, Dear . . . " *Today's Christian Woman.* Vol. 24, No. 2 (March/April 2002): 68.

Daring Greatly: How the Courage to Be Vulnerable Transforms the Way We Live, Love, Parent, and Lead. http://www.goodreads.com/author/quotes/162578.Bren_Brown?page=2 http://www.goodreads.com/quotes/tag/broken

Feldhahn, Shaunti. *For Women Only: What You Need to Know about the Inner Lives of Men.* Sisters, OR: Multnomah Books, 2004.

Gilder, George. *Men and Marriage.* New York: Pelican Publishing, 1986.

Gray, John. *Men Are from Mars, Women Are from Venus.* New York: Reed Business Information, Inc., 1992

Harley, Jr., Ph.D., Willard. "Marriage Builders,"—*Successful Marriage Advice.* http://www.marriagebuilders.com/graphic/mbi3300_needs.html/. [July 9, 2009].

Harper, Hill. *The Conversation.* New York: Penguin Group, 2009.

Harvey, Steve. *Act Like a Lady, Think Like a Man: What Men Really Think About Love, Relationships, Intimacy, and Commitment.* New York: Amistad, 2009.

The Holy Bible King James Version: King James Version Economy. Peabody, MA: Hendrickson Publishers, 2004.

Lesser, Elizabeth. *Broken Open: How Difficult Times Can Help Us Grow.* New York: Villard, 2005.

Pitts, Gena. *Pro-Sports Wives Magazine.* December 2009.

Popenoe, David, and Whitehead, Barbara. "The State of Our Unions: The Social Health of Marriage in America." *The National Marriage Project, Why Men Won't Commit.* http://www.virginia.edu/marriageproject/specialreports/[Sept. 26, 2009].

Tolle, Eckhart. *A New Earth: Awakening to Your Life's Purpose.* New York: Walker and Co., 2008.

Williamson, Marianne. AUDIO FROM *A Course in Miracles,* Lesson 193, By Marianne Williamson, *Oprah Radio* | July 10, 2008.

• • •

Quote for Wendy Plump came from *Vow: A Memoir of Marriage (and other Affairs),* http://www.goodreads.com/quotes/tag/infidelity?page=4

Quote for Scott Dikkers came from *You Are Worthless: Depressing Nuggets of Wisdom Sure to Ruin Your Day,* http;//www.goodreads.com/author/quotes/58557.Scott_Dikkers

Afterword

Dear Reader,

Thank you so much for allowing us to express our opinions and share our stories with you. If you would like to arrange for speaking engagements or share your thoughts, please feel free to contact us at info@lovingme1st.com or visit our Website at www.lovingme1st.com, where more up-to-date information is available. We are also on Facebook and Twitter.

God Bless,

Shanae and Rhonda

Notes